REPRODUCTION

OF

SOUND

by Edgar Villchur

ACOUSTIC RESEARCH, INC., *Cambridge, Massachusetts*

DOVER PUBLICATIONS, INC., *New York*

DEDICATION

To my wife, Rosemary, and my daughter, Miriam

Published in Canada by General Publishing Company, Ltd., 30 Lesmill Road, Don Mills, Toronto, Ontario.
Published in the United Kingdom by Constable and Company, Ltd., 10 Orange Street, London W. C. 2.

This Dover edition, first published in 1965, is a revised and enlarged republication of the work first published by Acoustic Research, Inc., 24 Thorndike Street, Cambridge, Massachusetts 02141, in 1962.

Standard Book Number: 486-21515-6
Library of Congress Catalog Card Number: 65-26018

Manufactured in the United States of America

Dover Publications, Inc.
180 Varick Street
New York, N. Y. 10014

TABLE OF CONTENTS

INTRODUCTION

INTRODUCTION

SOME YEARS AGO Mr. C. G. McProud, editor and publisher of *Audio,* called me. He asked me to write a series of articles for *Audio* which would survey the field as a previous *Audio* series of mine had done. This time, he said, leave out all equations, mathematical analyses, and material based on previous technical knowledge. He asked me to write the series in such a way that it would make sense to a novice, assuming intelligent and patient reading.

Mr. McProud's call resulted in a series of articles that appeared in twelve successive issues of *Audio.* I have now revised these articles, brought them up to date (stereo, for example, is included as an integral part), and they are presented here together.

What I have tried to do is to give the reader an intuitive, physical understanding of the nature of sound and of how the different parts of a reproducing system work. Mathematical details can follow later in more detailed study, if desired. This book may be thought of as a survey of principles for the interested layman, or as a pre-engineering survey and introduction for those who will become professionals.

I would like to express my appreciation to *Audio* magazine for the permission granted to Acoustic Research to publish these articles in book form, and to the *Saturday Review* for permission to use (in chapter 2) part of an article of mine published in that magazine in 1961. Finally, since I have not used footnote references, I would like to acknowledge the deep indebtedness of this work to the body of audio and acoustical literature on which it leans so heavily.

1.

SOUND

IT IS COMMON KNOWLEDGE that the generation of sound is associated with mechanical vibration, although the exact nature of this vibration, and the way in which it communicates itself to our ears, is not as widely understood. Newton referred to sources of sound as "tremulous bodies." This is an apt expression, because it implies a to-and-fro motion which is small, fast, and constantly repeated.

The vibrations of stretched strings, reeds, or membranes are familiar examples of such motion. When the vibrating body advances it pushes against the air with which it is in contact, compressing the molecules in front of it. Force applied to a rigid body would cause the whole body to move like a piston, all parts in unison, but an essential characteristic of an acoustic medium is that it is elastic. The molecules of air, therefore, are instead propelled against their neighboring particles, which in turn transmit the pressure to *their* neighbors, and a pressure impulse moves out with a definite speed from the original disturbance. When the source retreats it draws the nearby air towards it; the resulting partial vacuum is filled in by particles further out, and this time a rarefaction impulse travels out from the source.

Thus we have an impulse, alternately of compression and of rarefaction, which moves out from the oscillating source and which controls the behavior of the particles in its path, causing them first to crowd together and then to spread apart. A given particle imitates the to-and-fro motion of the source, but with a time lag, like that between the leader and followers of a "Simple Simon says" game. The time lag grows progressively greater with distance, and since the pressure changes are spread over an increasingly larger area, as the sound impulse moves out the imitative vibrations of the air molecules become weaker.

The vibrations of a source of sound are small: they may cover as much as a sizable fraction of an inch. But the human ear can detect particle "excursions" of microscopic distances—as little as .0001 inches—and it can detect changes of pressure of the order of magnitude that would be created by raising or lowering a body in the earth's atmosphere about one foot.

Sound travels as a "wave," and hence the transmission is accomplished without permanent displacement of air. This transmission can only take place through an elastic medium, a fact which was finally demonstrated by the classical experiment in which a bell and clapper were placed in an evacuated glass jar. The bell's vibrations were made inaudible, as sound could not be transmitted through the vacuum.

If the moon is ever visited one feature of its environment will be known beforehand with certainty; the wastes will be noiseless except for ·vibrations transmitted through the solid surface. Since there is no gaseous atmosphere there can be no tread of footsteps heard, no rustle of clothing, and if an obstruction is dynamited the débris will fly apart silently, as in a dream.

When a stone is dropped into a pool of water, waves travel out in all directions. This phenomenon is often used as an analogy to the action of sound waves. The force of the dropped stone is sent out through the water, but the particles of water merely vibrate in orderly sequence and do not travel with the force. There is an important difference, however, between this type of wave motion and that of sound. The particles of water vibrate up and down, in a direction approximately transverse to the direction of wave travel, rather than back and forth along the path of the wave (as they would if they were transmitting sound). The water wave is thus called *transverse*, the sound wave *longitudinal*.

It is easy to draw a picture of a transverse wave which will reveal its characteristics; we merely take a cross-sectional side view of the medium at any particular moment. It is more complicated, however, to make a pictorial representation of a longitudinal sound wave. We would have to show the particles alternately compressed and rarefied, as in (A) of *Fig.* 1-1, and since we could only show a few particles the picture would be a crude one. Therefore we abandon pictorial representation and substitute a symbolic graph, as in (B) of *Fig.* 1-1. Where the graph line crosses the horizontal axis the medium is in its normal, undisturbed state; where the graph reaches its peak height the medium is compressed to a maximum degree; and where the graph reaches the bottom of its trough the medium is at maximum rarefaction.

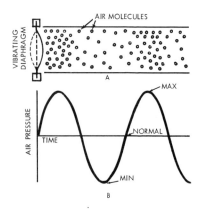

Fig. 1-1. (A) Alternate compression and rarefaction of air caused by sound. (B) The physical picture of (A) represented symbolically by a graph.

This graph represents the pressure state of the medium at a given point, as it varies over a period of time. We must always remember that these graph "wave forms" are not pictorial, and that, unlike ocean waves, sound waves do not physically look like their graph curves. The ocean wave actually forms such a pattern in space because of the fact that its particles vibrate transversely.

The Characteristics of a Sound Wave

The adoption of the above method for graphically representing sound waves makes an analysis of the quality of a sound much easier. A person would never mistake a buzz-saw for an oboe, but the differences can also be detected by an oscilloscope and stated in purely quantitative terms. The graph of pressure vs. time will tell the story if we know how to read it.

First, consider the height of the graph, from peak to trough. The greater the vertical distance the more the air is being compressed and rarefied, the greater the excursion forced on the ear drum, and the greater will be the intensity of the sound. This characteristic is called *amplitude*.

The second significant characteristic of the graph is the number of times per second the complete sequence of vibratory events, called *cycles*, occurs. This characteristic is referred to as the *frequency*, and the sensation of pitch depends on it. The higher the frequency the higher the pitch. But all sounds do not have pitch, as is evident from listening to many of the everyday sounds of the street. The existence of a definite pitch requires that a number of successive cycles of the same frequency be repeated. Regularity of this nature makes the sound a *periodic* one. Nonperiodic sounds are produced by automobiles, by leaves in the wind, or by the jangle of keys on a ring, and are referred to as noises rather than musical tones. Periodic sounds are produced by musical instruments—middle *C* on the piano, for example, represents a string vibration whose frequency is approximately 261 cycles per second (abbreviated as 261 cps). The frequency range of audible sound for a normal young person is about 20 cps to 20,000 cps.

The third feature which must be taken into account is the shape of the graph, or the *wave form*, which determines timbre. The graph of *Fig.* 1-1 is that of a sound created by the simplest of vibrations. It is called a sine wave. It is found relatively rarely in nature and has a tone which has little interest musically. The tone produced by blowing across the top of a bottle is usually of this type, except for its noise component. The characteristic timbre of various musical sounds is associated with a characteristic wave form, and it is this element which will immediately allow us to differentiate the oscilloscope pattern of one sound from another.

The reproduction of the tones of a whole symphony orchestra by a single vibrating speaker cone becomes less of a miracle when we understand the full significance of the wave form of sound. The wave form graph, besides representing the instantaneous pressure state of the air, may also be thought of as representing the instantaneous position of the human ear drum receiving the sound. It is obvious that, no matter how many sounds from how many instruments are being heard at the same time, the ear drum can be in only one position at any particular instant. Since we are able to hear and distinguish many sounds at once, evidently the single, complex vibration, and a single complex wave form can represent a combination of many different sounds. An oscilloscope picture of the wave form of the total sound of a symphony orchestra would be formed by a complicated but single line, and a headset diaphragm could theoretically reproduce exactly the same ear drum vibration as 75 musical instruments playing together.

A fourth characteristic of sound is more subtle but not of less importance. It has to do with the instantaneous changes of volume which take place, especially those involved in the starting and stopping of the sound. The wave characteristic which defines this element is called the wave envelope, and it describes the transient attack and decay of a tone, one type of vibrato, and crescendo and diminuendo.

The physical characteristics of sound listed above—the amplitude of the pressure changes, the frequency, the wave form, and the wave envelope—are associated with the sensations of loudness, pitch, timbre, and the sensation inspired by instantaneous amplitude changes, in that order. This is illustrated in *Fig.* 1-2.

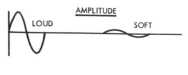

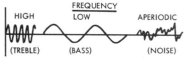

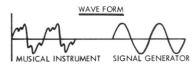

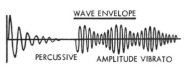

Fig. 1-2. The four physical characteristics of sound.

Although these associations are primarily correct the sensations are not each determined exclusively by one physical characteristic. Loudness is also affected by pitch, pitch by loudness, timbre by wave envelope, and so on.

Musical Instruments

The sound quality of a musical instrument, which we describe with subjective terms such as "fiery," "melancholy," "brilliant," etc., can also be described in terms of the four physical characteristics of sound referred to above.

The most dramatic characteristic of an instrument is its *timbre*, which we have seen is primarily associated with wave form. Musical instruments vibrate in complex ways; in addition to vibrating at the frequency corresponding to

the musical note on the score, they also vibrate simultaneously at many other, higher frequencies. The basic tone which identifies the pitch is called the *fundamental*, while the higher frequency components are called *overtones*. It is the particular combination of fundamental and overtones, in number, kind, and relative amplitude, that determines the wave form and the timbre.

In most musical instruments the overtone frequencies are simple multiples of the fundamental frequency. Such overtones are called *harmonics*. Thus if the fundamental tone is *A* above middle *C*, 440 cps, the second harmonic will be 880 cps, the third harmonic 1320 cps, and so forth. The general musical term for any component of a sound, whether fundamental or not, is *partial*.

The wave form and make-up of the complex musical tone of a violin, showing both the fundamental and harmonic overtones, is illustrated in *Fig.* 1-3.

Not all musical instruments, however, have overtones that are harmonic. Certain instruments of the orchestra, as a matter of fact, simultaneously produce such a varied assortment of harmonically unrelated frequencies that there is no definite sensation of one pitch. Strike tones and inharmonic overtones make up a large part of the sound of such members of the percussive group as the triangle, the bass drum, and the cymbals.

It is also true that certain musical tones, with harmonic overtones, have weak and even inaudible fundamentals. The lowest strings of the piano are examples. We nevertheless clearly identify the pitch correctly, because we recognize the harmonic structure and we respond to the *difference frequency* between harmonics (which, of course, is always the fundamental frequency). This phenomenon of hearing accounts for the fact that tones from the double bass or organ pedal pipes, when reproduced by table-model radios which are incapable of vibrating at the low funda-

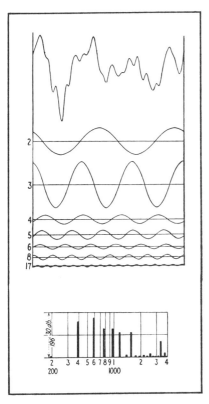

Fig. 1-3. Wave form and harmonic composition of a violin tone (G below middle C). (After Seashore)

mental frequencies involved, can still be recognized musically.

Musical instruments also differ widely in relation to the three characteristics of sound other than timbre. The majesty of the full pipe organ is partly due to its ability to pump very large quantities of vibrating air from its pipes, and to achieve tremendous volumes of sound. Some instruments, such as the pipe organ and piano, cover the entire musical range of fundamental frequencies, while others are specifically designed for bass or treble passages. The attack and decay of musical instruments may be character-

ized by sharp attack and slow decay, giving the sound a percussive quality, or by a gradual rise and fall of volume.

Units of Measurement

There are two units of measurement in sound that should not be omitted from this discussion. One is the musical pitch interval—the octave, whole tone, etc.—and the other is the engineering unit used to measure sound power, the decibel. Both are basically the same in concept.

A piano keyboard seems to be divided up evenly as far as pitch is concerned. The same apparent rise in pitch is produced by going from middle C to the next higher C, then to the C following, and so on, or from C to D to E. The first mentioned musical interval is called an *octave*, the second a *whole tone*. From C to C sharp is a *half tone*.

This apparently even division does not correspond to a similarly uniform physical division of frequency. As we increase the musical pitch, octave by octave, we are not adding equal increments of cycles, but are instead multiplying the frequency by two. Starting at 440 cps, one octave up will take us to 880 cps; two octaves up will take us not to 1320 cps but 1760 cps. A musical interval thus represents a geometric *ratio* of frequency, not a given number of cycles. An octave at the bottom of the keyboard covers only 27.5 cps, while an octave at the upper end covers 2093 cps. The range of musical pitch, however, is the same for the two, because this is the way we perceive sound.

The decibel is a similar unit of ratio, except that it refers to sound power, and the basic multiplier in the db system is 10 rather than 2.

We could construct in our mind's eye a special keyboard instrument in which all keys played the same frequency, and where ascending the "scale" increased only the volume of the sound. This hypothetical instrument could be calibrated in decibels by designing it so that every ten keys increased the sound power ten times. For example, if .01 watt were produced by a given key, ten keys further up would produce .1 watt, and ten keys further, 1 watt. Each such group of ten keys would correspond to a power ratio of one *bel,* while each adjacent key would increase or decrease the power by one *decibel.*

Here, then, are some simple definitions: a bel is a power ratio of ten to one; a decibel is a power ratio of 1.259 to 1.

One decibel or db represents, under certain conditions, the minimum difference in sound power that the average human ear can perceive. There are conditions (such as at the lower frequencies) when several decibels of change are required for a person to notice the change of volume, and there are also conditions in which a small fraction of a decibel can be perceived.

The main reason for the adoption of the decibel system is the same as the reason for the octave system in music:

that's the way we hear, in terms of geometric ratio rather than arithmetic increments. Thus if we want to plot the performance of an audio component over the frequency spectrum, and require a graph which lays out the ranges of frequency with the proper importance assigned to each range, we imitate the piano keyboard and use a geometric scale. When we describe the output of this component at different frequencies we state variations in relative db units, rather than in absolute units such as watts. The former is more accurate in terms of perception, and hence more meaningful.

The similarity between the layout of a piano keyboard and of frequency response graph paper used in audio work is illustrated in *Fig.* 1-4. A comparison between a numerical and decibel scale of power is illustrated in *Fig.* 1-5.

We have discussed the decibel as a unit of relative sound power; it is also used as a unit of relative electrical power, or it can be applied to such quantities as voltage, current, sound

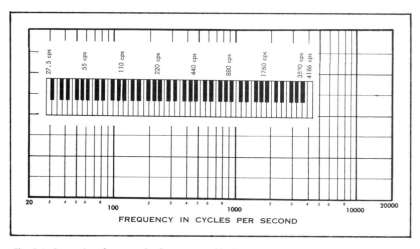

Fig. 1-4. Comparison between the frequency scale of a piano keyboard and that of an audio frequency response graph. The horizontal scale of the graph and the keyboard of the piano are each laid out according to frequency ratios.

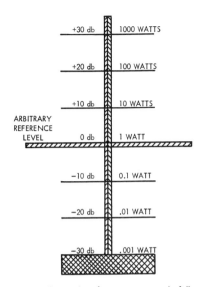

+30 db   1000 WATTS

+20 db   100 WATTS

+10 db   10 WATTS

ARBITRARY
REFERENCE
LEVEL   0 db   1 WATT

−10 db   0.1 WATT

−20 db   .01 WATT

−30 db   .001 WATT

Fig. 1-5. Comparison between a numerical (in this case geometric) power scale and a decibel power scale.

pressure, and sound intensity (power per unit area). When a level of sound is described in db a reference level is always given or assumed.

Resonance

Resonance is the basis of musical instrument design; it also plays an important but usually unwelcome role in sound reproducing systems.

If we pluck a stretched piano string it will vibrate for a while at a certain frequency. If we try it again we will find that the fundamental frequency is the same. This frequency is its natural or *resonant* frequency.

When the string is first released it is in a position of stretch, and it springs back. But when it has straightened itself out it is moving transversely at high speed, and momentum carries it beyond its neutral position, into a position of stretch on the other side. The overshoot is stopped by an opposing elastic restoring force, and the same half-cycle of

events begins again, this time in the opposite direction.

It may be seen that the original energy injected into the system is not absorbed by either the elastic or the mass element, but is stored temporarily by each in turn, and is poured back and forth from one to the other. The rate of interchange of this energy, which is to say the resonant frequency of the system, is determined by the relative values of mass and elasticity of the string. This is why the strings of the piano become progressively heavier as the pitch decreases, and why tightening the strings of a violin, which increases their elastic restoring force, raises the frequency of the tone produced.

The vibrations cannot go on indefinitely, because energy is lost with each excursion—partly through mechanical and acoustical friction, and partly through the energy represented by the radiated sound. If no new stimulus is given to the string, each overshoot becomes less than the previous one, until the system has come to rest. The process of energy absorption which brings motion to a halt is called *damping*. Heavy damping stifles the sound quickly, while a relatively undamped system allows the tone to continue for a long period of time.

The restoring force of a freely vibrating mechanical system may be supplied by gravity as well as by elasticity, as it is in the case of a suspended pendulum or of water sloshing about in a washbowl.

Forced vibrations are of a different character. The stimulating energy cannot be a one-shot affair but must be applied continuously, and the vibrating element follows the dictates of the stimulus rather than of its own resonant tendencies. But all mechanical systems have mass and restoring force to some extent; there is no such thing as a massless body or perfect rigidity. The loudspeaker, too, has its own resonant characteristics which we cannot exorcise even though we might like to. A system subjected to forced oscillation acts differently when the frequency of the stimulus comes close to or coincides with the natural frequency of the system itself. It offers much less resistance (technically the term is impedance) to being vibrated, and as a consequence the oscillatory excursions are very much greater than they are at other frequencies, even though the magnitude of the stimulating force has not changed.

Thus when a recorded bass viol sounds a tone which happens to be at the resonant frequency of the phonograph's loudspeaker, there is a tendency for that particular tone to "boom." Fortunately there are ways to mitigate and even to completely overcome this tendency.

A dramatic example of the results of resonant behavior is given in the description, according to one theory of geophysics, of the formation of the moon. The entire surface of the originally molten earth, it is stated, followed a tidal ebb and flow created by the gravitational influence of the sun, which alternately, according to the rotational position of the planet, caused the surface to lead and lag its spinning core. (The day was then about four hours instead of twenty-four). We can recognize the situation as one of forced oscillation of an inertia-gravity system, whose frequency was controlled by the velocity of rotation of the earth about its axis. This velocity began to decrease, due to frictional losses incurred with each tidal shift of the surface. It is reasoned that at some point the frequency of tidal oscillation coincided with the resonant frequency of the terrestrial mechanical system or of some part of it; the surface excursions reached their peak of violence, and a part of the surface was broken loose and hurled into space.

Another example of the effect of resonance on forced vibrations is the "wolf-note" produced in certain stringed instruments such as the cello. The body of the instrument, forced into vibration by the bowed string, has its own natural modes of oscillation, which help form the characteristic tone of the instrument. An unfortunate design may cause the excursions of belly and back to over-vibrate at their primary resonant frequency. Pieces do not fly off, but the howling sound produced has the unpleasant connotations of its name.

Acoustical Resonant Sources

There are also sources of an acoustical nature in which free vibrations may be induced. These fall into two types; the air column, such as exists in the flute, pipe organ or "acoustical labyrinth" loudspeaker enclosure, and the Helmholtz resonator, illustrated by the empty bottle, the ocarina, or the bass-reflex speaker enclosure.

The simpler of these two is the Helmholtz resonator. It consists of an en-

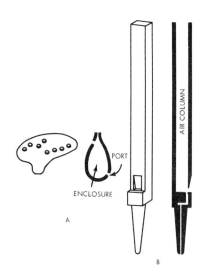

Fig. 1-6. Helmholtz and air column resonance, illustrated by simplified diagrams of ocarina and flue organ pipe.

closed body of air with an opening or duct to the outside. If the longest acoustic path within the enclosed space is small relative to the wave length of a stimulating oscillation, the internal pressure state at any instant will not vary significantly from one point to another, and the entire bulk of the imprisoned air will be compressed and rarefied as a unit.

The enclosed air supplies elasticity, and the requirements of a freely oscillating system (restoring force and inertia) are completed by the acoustic mass of the air in the port or duct. A close mechanical analogy would be a weight on a spring.

The Helmholtz resonator is characterized by the fact that it produces no harmonics, and that its natural frequency is determined by the dimensions of the port and the *volume* (not length) of the enclosure.

The resonant frequency of the air column, on the other hand, is determined precisely by the length of the column, and it is rich in harmonic overtones. The air can pulsate longitudinally as a whole, in sections, or in both modes simultaneously. It should be clear from the comparative characteristics of these two resonant devices that the air column is the one most suitable for musical instruments. *Fig.* 1-6 illustrates both resonators, as used in the ocarina and in the organ pipe.

2.

STANDARDS OF HIGH FIDELITY

IT MIGHT APPEAR that following a discussion of the nature of sound, the logical subject to consider would be the criteria for reproducing this sound with "high fidelity" to the original. One other element, however, should be covered first—the way in which we hear.

Perception of Sound

We have already seen, in examining units of measurement for pitch and power—the octave and the decibel—that our perception of sound does not necessarily correspond directly to the objective reality. The illusion is consistent, however, so that a given sound always has the same effect on a normal ear.

An important element in the perception of sound was discovered by Fletcher and Munson in 1933. These investigators demonstrated that our impression of loudness did not depend solely on the amplitude of the sound wave, but on other things as well. Specifically, they showed that sound in the lower treble range of the frequency spectrum—the 3500-cps region—appeared to be much louder than sound of the same amplitude

at any other part of the spectrum. Thus, if the frequency scale was swept by a tone which continuously rose in frequency but kept exactly the same amplitude, the *loudness,* or apparent amplitude, would increase to a maximum at about 3500 cps and then fall off again.

This fact does not have much practical interest for the person listening to reproduced music, except as it describes the relative nuisance value of different types of noise. No matter how lop-sided our interpretation of acoustic reality, we make the same interpretation in the concert hall as in our living room, and the craftsmen who designed musical instruments (who worked to satisfy their ears, not sound-level meters) perceived sound in the same way.

Fletcher and Munson made a second discovery, however, that does bear directly on the reproduction of sound. They found that the effect described above took place in varying degree, depending on the over-all level of the sound. For very high amplitude sound the drop in loudness with frequency below 3500 cps hardly occurred at all, while for very soft sound the effect was maximum. Above 3500 cps the effect remained constant, within 2 or 3 db, no matter what the over-all sound level.

The well-known "equal loudness contours," also referred to as the Fletcher-Munson curves, are reproduced in *Fig.* 2–1. Each curve plots the sound amplitude required to produce the same perceived loudness at different frequencies of the scale. It can be seen that normal hearing losses in the bass end become progressively greater as the over-all sound level is decreased.

This means that if an orchestra plays a musical passage at the sound level represented by 90 db, and if this music is reproduced at the 60 db level, we will hear the bass with less *relative* loudness than we would have heard it at the concert itself. If you follow the 90- and 60-db curves, shown superimposed in *Fig.* 2–2, you will see that there is approximately a 14 db perceived loss at 50 cps—it takes 14 db more of actual amplitude, in the lower curve, to produce the same relative loudness at 50 cps as it does in the upper curve.

In order to re-create the original balance of perceived frequencies at low volume levels, it has become customary to introduce bass boost which is related to the setting of the volume control, either automatically or otherwise.

A volume control tied to automatic bass boost is called a *loudness control.* (Some loudness controls also boost the treble spectrum appreciably at low volume settings. There is no justification for this in the Fletcher-Munson curves.)

High Fidelity to What?

The assumption will be made here that the purpose of high fidelity equipment is to reproduce as closely as possible the experience of the concert hall, not to transcend or improve it.

I remember an exhibition at New York's Museum of Modern Art, during the late thirties, of "high fidelity" reproductions of water color paintings. Life-size reproductions were hung side by side with the originals, and it was often difficult or impossible to tell them apart. There was no question in anyone's mind about how to judge the quality of these prints. The only criterion was accuracy. The public that visited the exhibit was used to looking at paintings, and was able to make an immediate comparison

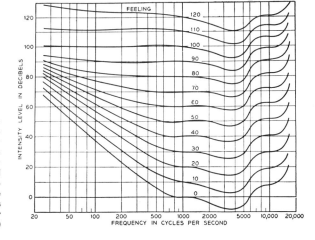

Fig. 2-1. The Fletcher-Munson equal loudness contours. For each curve, the height at any point represents the sound amplitude required to produce the same subjective loudness as at 1000 cps. (After Fletcher and Munson)

11

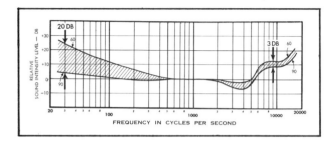

Fig. 2-2. The 60 and 90 db Fletcher-Munson curves superimposed. The shaded area represents the difference in normal hearing loss from one sound level to the other.

between the copy and the original. No one thought of the prints as entities in themselves, with qualities independent of the qualities of the originals.

This point of view does not always hold in the field of high fidelity musical reproduction. Only a minority of today's high fidelity public are concert-goers. Many have never attended a live concert; they know the sound of the orchestra or of individual musical instruments only as it is reported by amplifiers and loudspeakers. They may know what they like in reproduced sound, but they have no way of evaluating the realism of reproduction.

This partly explains why so much variation is tolerated in audio equipment. The same record may sound very different when played through different brands of equipment, each brand equally acceptable in the market place. The evaluation of high fidelity components is popularly thought of as an entirely subjective matter, like comparing the tone of one violin to that of another rather than like holding a facsimile up to its original.

For similar reasons high fidelity demonstrations such as the annual Hi-Fi shows can get away with a lot of sound that is startling but essentially non-musical. Some of the "reproduced" sound that greets the show visitor is necessarily unfamiliar because it has no live counterpart. A harmonica blown up in volume to the dimensions of a theatre organ is a new and different instrument. A

crooner whispering into a microphone an inch away invents a new sound; his unamplified voice is never heard in public. A combination of Bongo drum, chimes and electric guitar creates a *tutti* which one may like or dislike, but for which there is no equivalent in one's memory to serve as a live standard.

Such sound can only be accepted as a self-sufficient entity, like an old calendar chromo. Any resemblance to live music or to painting is purely coincidental, and the science and/or art of *re*production is not really involved.

High fidelity has undoubtedly increased rather than decreased the ranks of music lovers, and there are probably more people than ever who are unimpressed with gimmick sound. Many designers and manufacturers in the field work only for naturalness of reproduction. The designer of integrity avoids like the plague those exaggerations that sometimes attract the novice—over-emphasized bass for "depth," over-emphasized mid-range for "presence," over-emphasized treble for "brilliance." These distortions are more properly called, respectively, boominess, nasality or "honkiness," and harshness.

Many demonstrations are not, fortunately, of the gimmick type, and use musical material played at musical levels. There have also been concerts staged with live musicians, in which direct comparisons of reproduced sound to the sound of the live instruments could be made, in the same way that direct comparisons of prints to original paintings were made at the Museum of Modern Art. The live vs. recorded public concert is one method of giving direction to equipment designers and perspective to high fidelity consumers. Although transferring concert hall atmosphere to the home has special problems of its own, success in creating an identity of sound in the concert hall itself solves the major part of the problem. Even more vital to maintaining balance and perspective in the high fidelity world is live concert attendance.

We are now prepared to discuss the technical standards of quality that may be applied to a sound reproducing system. There will be no dividing lines proposed, at which low fidelity becomes medium, high, or super.

Frequency Response

The frequency response of a sound reproducing system, or of one of its components, describes its relative handling of parts of the input signal which differ in frequency. "Handling" may refer to electrical amplification, as in an amplifier, to conversion of mechanical to electrical energy, as in a pickup, or to conversion from electrical to acoustical energy, as in a loudspeaker.

There are two aspects of frequency response: the *range* of frequencies handled, and the *uniformity* with which the unit or system responds to different frequencies. Knowledge of the first of these is useless without knowledge of the second. Let us therefore pass over the question of range for the moment, and determine what uniformity will be required for the range we finally decide on.

Uniformity of Response

Although the trained ear can usually perceive a change of sound level of a db or less in test signals, the average observer is probably less sensitive to a change of sound level in a particular frequency range of a musical passage.

Reproduction which remains constant over its frequency range within one or two db would thus probably be adequate for perfect apparent fidelity, other things being equal.

This standard can be met in amplifiers without much difficulty, even at high power levels. The best pickups are also able to conform, but loudspeakers are laggard in this respect.

The results of non-uniform reproduction are several. Undue volume in a particular section of the sound spectrum can produce stridency or boominess as opposed to natural musical sound. More particularly, the existence of sharp peaks in the response curve, usually representing a resonant condition, mean that *hangover* or *ringing* may be present— the speaker cone or section of cone will continue to vibrate after the signal has stopped. This is perceived as a "rain-barrel" effect, a muddying up of the sound and impairment of the distinctness of the different instrumental voices. Such an effect is also indicated when the listener is unable to distinguish clearly the pitch of low-frequency tones.

Another important effect of peaked frequency response is the exaggeration of unwanted noise components such as turntable rumble or record surface scratch. This effect was not given its due recognition in the earlier days of high fidelity, when the existence of rumble and surface noise was proudly displayed as evidence of extended frequency range.

The amount of surface noise in a good quality modern LP record and the amount of rumble from a good record player are such that there will not be much significant noise produced in a system with uniform frequency response, even though the frequency range be extended to the limits of the present state of the art. In a comparison test conducted recently between two tweeters, the one which was able to reproduce almost an octave more of treble (into the inaudible region) showed a dramatic decrease of surface noise, due to its extreme evenness of response. There was no selective reproduction of discrete frequency regions, and the switch to the superior speaker produced a fuller, more natural treble simultaneously with the reduction in surface noise.

A similar situation exists with regard to turntable rumble. A peaked system whose response falls off rapidly below 60 cps may exhibit more turntable rumble than a smooth system whose full response extends an octave lower.

Tell-tale evidence of the existence of peaked reproduction in the bass may be gathered from listening to the reproduction of speech. The male speaking voice ordinarily contains no sound components whose frequency is below 100 cps, and the reproducing system should give no hint (by a boomy, resonant quality in the voice) that it is also capable of speaking in the tones of the double bass.

Range of Response

It is generally agreed among acoustics authorities that the range of 40 to 15,000 cps is sufficient for perfect or near-perfect apparent fidelity in the reproduction of orchestral music. The phrase "near-perfect" is meant to imply that when such a range has been achieved the designer should direct his attention to inaccuracies of reproduction more gross than are associated with the frequency limitations indicated.

For the pipe organ enthusiast, however, there is significant intelligence (significant, that is, from the point of view of the emotional impact of the music) down to 32 cps or lower. 32.7 cps is three octaves below middle C relative to A-440, and is the lowest note of the average pipe organ, although many larger organs reach down an octave lower. These low organ tones are distinguished by the fact that they contain a strong fundamental component. The lowest tones of the piano, on the other hand, contain no fundamental energy that significantly affects the quality of the sound. Even though the lowest key on the piano strikes 27.5 cps, response down to this frequency is not required for the reproduction of piano music.

Probably no characteristic of audio components is so freely booted about by advertising copywriters as frequency range. Any numerical range of frequencies listed is totally meaningless unless accompanied by a description of the decibel tolerance above or below reference that is being used, and, for a loudspeaker, by a description of off-axis response as well. A 3-in. speaker made for portable radios will "respond" when stimulated by a 30-cps signal—perhaps by having its cone tear loose and fly out into the air—and almost any speaker, even a woofer, will make some kind of sound when stimulated by a high-powered 15,000-cps signal. A frequency response rating must mean something more than that a signal of given frequency makes a speaker move audibly, or that it makes an amplifier show an electrical output of some sort at its terminals. It must mean that within a stated frequency range, and, for power devices, within a stated range of power, the fundamental output of a given device is uniform to a stated degree.

Treble Dispersion

The on-axis response of a loudspeaker may be very deceiving, because the higher frequencies tend to be directed in a beam which continually narrows as the frequency is raised. Good sound dispersion must therefore be a qualifying factor for any treble response curve.

A speaker which has relatively uniform treble output both on-axis and off-axis (over a reasonably large solid angle —perhaps 45 degrees in any direction from the axis) will reproduce music with a "spaciousness" that does not exist when there is more concentrated beaming of the treble. Furthermore, severely attenuated off-axis response in the treble means that the total sound power radiated at treble frequencies is considerably less than that implied by the on-axis response curve. It is this total radiated power, rather than the on-axis pressure, that determines whether a speaker will sound dull, natural, or over-bright in a normally reverberant room.

Transient Response

Transient response refers to the accuracy of reproduction of the wave envelope, and is concerned with the reproduction of attack and decay characteristics of the sound. We have seen that uniform frequency response predicts the absence of ringing; if the steady-state frequency response curve does not have peaks, the reproduced sound will die away just as in the original.

Consider, for example, the tone represented in (A) of *Fig.* 2–3. Perfect reproduction would produce an identical wave form, differing perhaps only in amplitude, while poor transient response would be indicated by the hangover that is apparent in (B). The continuation of the reproduced signal after the original

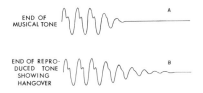

Fig. 2-3. Poor transient response.

has ended may be compared to a color smear on a reproduced painting.

Attack time involves the reproduction of frequencies higher than the fundamental. Although a percussive tone may have a low fundamental pitch, the frequency components associated with its steep attack characteristic may be very high. Natural reproduction of a drum

beat through a two-way speaker system may thus be accomplished by the "woofer" handling the fundamental tone and its proper decay, while the "tweeter" contributes the sound components that make up the sharp attack.

Harmonic and Intermodulation Distortion

Reproducing devices have a characteristic way of performing with less than perfect accuracy. In addition to the frequencies at which they are asked to vibrate mechanically (or alternate electrically) they introduce new modes of oscillation of their own—and these new frequencies are harmonics, integral multiples of the original frequency. This inaccuracy is called *harmonic distortion*. It is measured as the ratio of the amplitude of the spurious harmonics to the true signal, in per cent.

We have seen that harmonics of fundamental frequencies are produced in any case by musical instruments. Yet small amounts of harmonic distortion produce very unpleasant effects. The sound becomes harsh, unmusical; the bass is wooden and the treble painful.

The primary reason for this is that with harmonic distortion comes an attendant evil—intermodulation distortion. Intermodulation distortion can be described as the introduction of new sound components, at sum and difference frequencies, when tones of two or more frequencies are passed through a non-linear system—that is, a system which creates harmonic distortion. These sum and difference frequencies are harmonically unrelated to the original musical tones. They are musically discordant, and they serve to create raucous, unmusical sound in a degree proportional to their relative strength. The formation of intermodulation products is illustrated in *Fig.* 2–4.

The primary importance of low distortion has always been recognized by audio authorities. It has also become in-

15

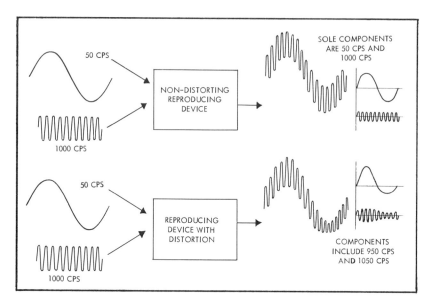

Fig. 2-4. Intermodulation distortion as a result of harmonic distortion of the low-frequency wave form. Note that the wave envelope of the high-frequency tone is "modulated."

creasingly recognized by the high fidelity public in recent years, after the first flush of excitement over reproducing regions of the frequency spectrum previously untouched. Amplifier manufacturers now feature distortion data over frequency response data; unfortunately it is very rare for loudspeaker specifications to make any quantitative reference to distortion at all. The reason lies in the fact that while both harmonic distortion and intermodulation distortion (the latter is usually greater by a factor of 3 or 4) can be kept to extremely low values in high quality amplifiers—a small fraction of one per cent at rated power—the corresponding values for loudspeakers are much higher. In the octave below 60 cps it is a rare speaker indeed which can hold harmonic distortion, at any appreciable sound level, below the 5 per cent mark over the entire octave, and many speakers produce percentages of distortion in this frequency region 'en

times as great. But the listening results are not as bad as might appear at first glance: speaker response is normally severely attenuated in this lower range, which helps, and there is comparatively little musical material of such low frequency to be distorted.

When the reproducing system has a minimum of low frequency distortion, very low bass tones of high power, such as might be produced by organ pedal pipes, not only remain pure in timbre themselves but do not create intermodulation with the rest of the music; they do not destroy the purity of the treble by introducing false tones.

Power Capability

The power capability of a high-quality reproducing system should be such as to be able to establish an intensity level of sound in the living room equal to the level at a good seat in the original concert hall. The electrical power required

16

of the amplifier for achieving this goal depends upon the efficiency of the speaker, and the sound power required of the speaker depends on the size and other acoustical characteristics of the room. Concert-hall level can be established in a living room with a tiny fraction of the acoustical power of a symphony orchestra, because the lower power is concentrated in a much smaller area.

"Concert-hall level" is sometimes misinterpreted to mean the sound level which would be created if the orchestra were somehow jammed into the living room itself. The writer has yet to experience at a live concert, even during *fortissimo* passages, an assault on his ears that compares to hi-fi assaults he has weathered. It is interesting to note that certain hi-fi demonstrations preclude intelligible conversation which is not shouted, while whispered conversations in a concert hall are liable to prove extremely distracting and annoying to one's neighbors. It is the sound intensity level at the ear, not the power of the orchestra, that we are trying to reproduce.

Noise Level

Any sound component not present in the original program material, other than distortion products, is referred to as noise, even though it may be periodic and not conform to our strictly scientific definition. Hum, rumble, surface scratch, tube hiss or other circuit noise and similar disturbances tend to destroy the auditory illusion, and must be kept to a minimum.

A standard for satisfactorily low noise has been established by the FCC for FM broadcast stations. It is that the power ratio of the maximum signal to the noise must always be at least 60 db; this represents a ratio of one million to one.

Dynamic Range

The dynamic range, or range of ampli-

tude of the reproduced sound from softest to loudest, is determined by the two factors just discussed, noise level and power capability.

Soft musical passages can be masked by any of the types of noise referred to, and therefore the lowest sound levels that can be used must be much louder than the noise level. The maximum sound levels that can be used, of course, are limited by the power capability of the system.

A dynamic range of 60 db, or a million to one power ratio between highest and lowest sound levels, is generally considered adequate for reproduction of the largest symphony orchestra.

Stereo

All of the above considerations apply equally to monaural and to stereophonic reproducing systems. These objective elements of equipment fidelity—low distortion, adequate frequency response, dynamic range, etc.—are able, in stereo, to contribute more to the subjective illusion of musical reality than in a monaural system.

A stereo record-reproduce system has in effect two parallel and complete monaural systems. The work of each component along the way is done twice. The sound is picked up by two separate microphones; the output of each microphone is recorded on a separate track of the tape; the record groove, although not doubled, is cut in such a way as to independently contain the record of each signal channel; the pickup contains two separate generating elements which independently sense and transmit each signal channel; the two signal outputs of the pickup are sent through independent amplifiers and fed to two independent loudspeakers. There are variations on this ideal scheme, but the above describes the basic concept of stereo.

The purpose of this dual-channel reproduction is, in the simplest terms, to help recreate the acoustical atmosphere of the concert hall. In the old-fashioned stereopticon each visual channel gave a slightly different perspective view of the subject. Similarly, in stereo recording, each microphone gets a slightly different auditory perspective. It is important to note that this auditory perspective is of the orchestra or soloists *in the hall* in which they are performing, not merely of the musical performers in the abstract. This is important because a good part of the sound that reaches our ears at a concert does not come directly from the orchestra, but is reflected from the walls and ceiling of the concert hall.

The channels of a stereo system are identified as "right and "left." This does not mean that one microphone picks up the sound of the right section of the orchestra only, and that the other microphone picks up the sound from the left section of the orchestra. It does mean that one microphone has a right-oriented perspective of the total sound in the recording hall, and that the other microphone has a left-oriented perspective of the total sound. When these two recorded channels (which, like the two photos on a stereopticon card, are very similar to each other) are reproduced through two separate loudspeakers they create, although not perfectly, the illusion of the acoustical environment and sense of space of the concert hall. There is an increased awareness of the physical position of different instruments, but this is very much less important than the general increase in realism and the consequent increase of clarity, particularly from the point of view of the distinctness of the different musical voices.

There is an approach to stereo recording, commonly referred to as "ping-pong" stereo, which provides an exaggerated separation between the right and left channels. If only the left side of the orchestra were playing during a particular passage, there would be practically no sound from the right recording channel. The left-right orientation of the different instruments is the primary goal in this case, rather than reproduction of the original acoustical environment. The degree to which one's attention is directed to the physical position of the instruments in "ping-pong" stereo is often much greater than that at the live concert itself.

The greatest benefit of good stereo recording and reproduction is that it frees us, to a greater extent than was possible previously, from the acoustical environment of the listening room, and transports us to some extent to the acoustical environment of the hall in which the recording was made. The normal living room does not provide the proper acoustical atmosphere for a musical concert, particularly of a large orchestra. Musical instrument designers worked in terms of the tonal qualities that would be produced in the type of concert hall with which they were familiar.

3.

THE SOUND REPRODUCING SYSTEM

THE PHONOGRAPH is a classic example of an invention that cannot be credited wholly to one man. In 1877 Edison directed his assistant, John Kruesi, to construct the first complete record-reproduce system, but sound recorders were sold on a commercial basis as early as 1860, and Thomas Young's "A Course of Lectures on Natural Philosophy" described and illustrated a crude but practical sound recorder in 1807.

Young's recorder consisted of a sharp metal stylus held by spring tension against a revolving cylinder, the cylinder coated with wax and turned by a governor-controlled gravity motor. When a vibrating body such as a tuning fork was held against the stylus, a wavy line was cut into the wax. This line represented the wave form of the vibrations, and it could be studied and analyzed at leisure. The recorder was a mechanical draftsman, that could sense very small motions and record pressure changes that took place within a period of a very small fraction of a second.

By 1856 Léon Scott de Martinville had constructed the "phonautograph"

(self-writer of sound) illustrated in *Fig.* 3–1. The sound wave form was scratched by a hog-bristle stylus on the surface of a cylinder coated with lamp-black, but the big advance over Young's machine was the fact that the phonautograph could record directly from the air. The force of the acoustical vibrations

Fig. 3-1. The phonautograph of Léon Scott de Martinville — a commercial sound recorder of the eighteen sixties. (Courtesy Smithsonian Institution)

was concentrated by a horn onto a diaphragm, and the stylus was attached to the diaphragm, so that the recording needle did not have to actually touch the vibrating source of sound. This device, which corresponds in function to the modern oscilloscope, was a catalogue item of the Paris firm of Koenig, and was sold as a measuring instrument to acoustical laboratories.

The phonautograph which is at the Smithsonian Institution at Washington would undoubtedly reproduce music if a proper record were placed on its revolving cylinder. The theoretical possibility of playback was understood then, too, but the lampblack records were useless for playback, as their grooves were not rigid enough to direct the vibrations of a playback needle. About half a year before Edison got his brainstorm Charles Cros conceived a method for bringing the groove sinuosities back to life as sound. The lampblack recording was to be photo-engraved on a metal cylinder, and running a needle through the hard groove would then cause the needle to vibrate from side to side, in the same time pattern as the hog bristle stylus that first inscribed the line.

For reasons which may be related to nineteenth century differences in tradition between the scholar and the industrial engineer, Cros didn't even construct a working model, but merely filed a complete, sealed description of his system with the *Académie des Sciences*. On the other hand, less than a month after Edison first conceived of a reproducing phonograph the country was reading about a working unit in newspaper headlines. There was a great stir of excitement over this amazing tonal imitator, (see *Fig. 3–2*) with public demonstrations, lectures before august scientific bodies, and a visit to the White House.

Fig. 3-2. Edison with his tin-foil phonograph. (Photograph by Brady — courtesy Smithsonian Institution)

The excitement soon died down, as the Edison machine was an impractical toy, with neither permanent records nor usable fidelity. The recorded groove was indented into a semi-hard material, tin foil; it was only able to retain its shape partially, and that for very few playings. Subsequent technical improvements, however, made the phonograph a popular device by the turn of the century. It is curious that our modern recording system, in which the record is a mechanical copy of the original master, is more closely related to Cros' system than to Edison's. Emil Berliner, the father of the moulded or cast record, began his research work by successfully carrying out Cros' proposals.

The Mechanical or "Acoustic" Phonograph

It would be useful to consider the design of the non-electric phonograph, as illustrated in (A) of *Fig. 3–3*. A better insight can thereby be gained into the function of the various components of a modern electronic system.

The wave forms frozen into the record groove control the vibrations of the playback stylus when the groove is dragged past the stylus by a revolving turntable. These stylus vibrations, although they contain a fairly large amount of mechanical energy, engage practically no air, like the revolutions of a bladeless electric fan. The needle is therefore attached to a diaphragm, which vibrates in sympathy with the stylus and has a much larger surface area in contact with the air of the room.

But even the reproducing diaphragm doesn't get a sufficient bite of the air for practical purposes. Therefore the diaphragm is placed at the narrow throat of an acoustical horn, and the actual usable sound emerges into the room from the much larger mouth of the horn. The system works somewhat as though the diaphragm area were really that of the horn's mouth.

It can be seen that all of the energy radiated by the horn is taken from the mechanical vibrations of the needle, and the forces between needle and record groove are necessarily great. This has obvious implications for record wear, but perhaps more important, the demands for power placed on the "sound box" or "speaker" (old-fashioned terms for the needle-diaphragm-head assembly) place a severe limitation on musical fidelity. High distortion and peaked and severely limited frequency response are to be expected.

The Phonograph Amplifier

The solution to this problem lies in changing the function of the phonograph pickup, from the primary generator of sound power to a device which controls an outside source of power. If the power from the outside source is made to oscillate in imitation of the needle vibrations, two benefits can result:

1. The final output sound derived

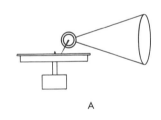

A

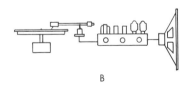

B

Fig. 3-3. (A) The mechanical phonograph. (B) The electric phonograph.

21

from the record groove can be much louder.

2. The power demands on the pickup itself are no longer heavy. The pickup can be designed for quality rather than loudness; the problems of achieving uniform, extended frequency response and low distortion are considerably lessened. So, incidentally, is the required weight on the pickup and the grinding away of the record groove.

The control of an outside source of power to conform to given oscillations is called *amplification*. The first phonograph amplifier was pneumatic: the needle was made to actuate an air valve, which periodically throttled a flow of compressed air. Most of the work of radiating sound power was thus performed by the air compressor, and the stylus was relieved of part of its burden.

All modern sound reproducing systems use amplifiers, but unlike the first pneumatic systems these amplifiers are electronic. The phonograph pickup is no longer a sound generator but an electric generator. It produces small alternating voltages at its terminals, whose wave forms conform to those of the groove and of the recorded sound. The pickup has to generate very little power, because the output voltage can be amplified to almost any desired degree. The amplified electrical power must finally, of course, be converted back into sound by a loudspeaker. The two types of reproducing system, electrical and purely mechanical, are shown in *Fig. 3—3*.

The Modern Sound Reproducing System

The purpose of the historical approach used above has been to furnish the reader with an appreciation of the reason for the modern audio system being designed as it is. With the electronic amplifier supplying the brute force, so to speak, the mechanical components—pickup and loudspeaker—can be built in such a way as to suppress the natural resonant tendencies inherent in mechanical vibratory systems.

Before discussing each of the audio components in detail, it would be useful to make a brief survey of the entire reproducing system. A complete monaural system is illustrated in *Fig. 3—4*.

First of all the disc record must be revolved by a *motor* and *turntable*. The chief operational requirements of this part of the system are that it revolve at the correct speed, that the speed be constant, and that extraneous vibrations do not communicate themselves to the pickup.

The first of these requirements is for the purpose of keeping the reproduced music at the same absolute pitch at which it was recorded: too fast a turntable speed will make the pitch sharp, and too low a speed will make it flat. The second condition listed, constant speed, is required in order to avoid pitch variations, or "wow." The third requirement, lack of extraneous vibrations, keeps low-frequency noise called "rumble" out of the final sound.

The groove variations are sensed by the *needle*, or *stylus*, which in high-quality systems is jewel tipped; it is usually diamond. The needle must have an unmarred, smooth surfaced, hard tip, normally of spherical shape.

The *pickup* is an electric generator (usually either of the piezo-electric, variable reluctance, or moving-coil type) whose function is to translate the mechanical vibrations of the needle into electrical oscillations of the same wave form. It must do this with minimum distortion of the wave form, and must not allow resonances of its own to influence its output voltage significantly. It is also an advantage for the pickup to impose as little work as possible on the needle. The greater the force required for the groove to displace the needle from side to side, the greater the vertical bearing force will have to be to

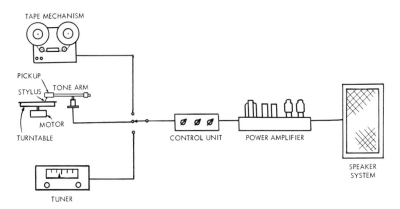

Fig. 3-4. Diagram of a complete monaural sound reproducing system.

maintain proper and constant stylus-groove contact, and the greater the wear of both record and needle.

The *tone arm* holds the pickup in place over the groove, and must provide sufficient freedom of motion so that the pressure of the groove walls alone can make the needle move across the record, following the recorded spiral. It must also be free enough to follow warp and eccentricity of the disc easily. The tone arm must hold the pickup approximately tangent to the groove being played, must provide the proper vertical force for the pickup, and must not allow its own resonant behavior to influence the system.

The electrical output of one type of pickup, the piezo-electric, is usually fed directly to the amplifier. It is of the order of $\frac{1}{2}$ volt or more, and is a fairly accurate replica of the recorded sound. This is so because the characteristic frequency response of the pickup is more or less the inverse image of the frequency characteristics "built in" to the record. (This last subject will be taken up in detail later.)

The reluctance and moving-coil pickups, however, produce a much smaller amount of electrical energy. The output

voltage of these pickups (which are classed together as *magnetic* types) may be as low as a few thousandths of a volt. Furthermore the characteristic frequency response of the magnetic pickup does not compensate for the way in which the frequency characteristics of the recorded sound has been doctored. Therefore the pickup output must be passed through a *preamplifier* before it enters the amplifier proper.

The preamplifier is normally combined with the main amplifier control sections (volume and tone controls). Its functions are to increase the output voltage of the pickup, and to compensate accurately for the frequency characteristics of the record so that the sound is not deficient in bass and heavy in the treble. Since different record companies have made records with different characteristics the preamplifier may allow the operator to choose between several types of frequency compensation. The need for such control, which is called variable record equalization, has disappeared with modern records, which are standardized on the RIAA recording characteristic.

The control section of the amplifier allows the operator to regulate the volume, and, in most cases, to either accentuate or attenuate ("boost" or "cut") the bass and treble portions of the reproduced sound independently. The primary function of tone control is to compensate for deficiencies in associated equipment or program material, and to compensate for acoustical conditions of the room in which the music is heard. When the control section and phonograph preamplifier are combined on one chassis, the entire unit is commonly referred to as a preamplifier.

The power amplifier receives the electrical signal as it is finally shaped, and releases another signal, ideally identical in all respects except power. The power amplification may be tens of millions of times, from a fraction of a microwatt (one millionth of a watt) to dozens of watts.

Although the demands on the amplifier are very great, and although it appears to be the most complicated of the system components, it is the least imperfect of these components. The percentages of harmonic and intermodulation distortion, the irregularities of frequency response, and the extraneous noise introduced by an amplifier built according to the best current design practice, and without regard for cost,

are such that they are not limiting factors in the fidelity of the reproduced sound.

The final component of the sound system is the loudspeaker system, which consists of the speaker mechanism itself and the speaker enclosure. The loudspeaker converts the alternating electrical output of the amplifier into mechanical vibrations of a cone or diaphragm. But the cone vibrating by itself cannot, for reasons that will be discussed further on, produce adequate bass energy. It must be mounted in an enclosure or baffle of some sort, which gives the vibrating surface the "bite" of air that it needs to radiate low-frequency sound.

The speaker and its enclosure, like the amplifier, should introduce as little distortion and frequency irregularity into the signal as possible. Typical speaker deficiencies are irregular frequency response, poor transient response (hangover), and harmonic and intermodulation distortion.

Two other components are shown in *Fig. 3–4*. The *tuner* is a device which converts AM or FM radio signals to audio signals that can be handled by the audio amplifier; the tape transport mechanism, with its associated pream-

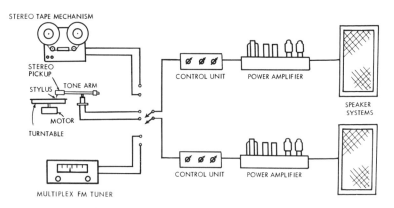

Fig. 3-5. A stereo reproducing system.

plifier, provides a signal of the same nature as that coming from the tuner or phonograph pickup.

Fig. 3-5 shows the basic elements of a stereo reproducing system. The stereo tape mechanism has two heads which independently reproduce each channel that is recorded in parallel on the tape; the stereo pickup provides two separate output signals from the two channels recorded in the groove (the turntable and pickup arm do not have to be dupli-cated); the stereo tuner receives the "multiplex" FM stereo signal and separates it into two separate channels, which it feeds independently to each of the control units. Each control unit and each power output is shown duplicated. The two control units and power amplifiers may be separate, or they may be combined on one chassis, or all four units may be combined on one chassis, but in any case they must provide independent amplification for each channel.

4.

DISC RECORDING

WE HAVE OUTLINED BRIEFLY the functions of each link in the chain of sound reproducing components, from pickup to speaker. It now remains to treat each of these components in some detail, and the reader may have been led to expect a discussion of pickups to follow the last chapter. But pickup design doesn't begin to make sense until the fundamental methods of disc recording are understood.

Variables in Disc Recording

In the earliest days of the commercial phonograph, when recording and reproducing the human voice was for stenographic rather than entertainment purposes, and when the same machine performed both the recording and the reproduction, standardization of record characteristics wasn't important. Records were matched to the playback equipment automatically. The introduction of the prerecorded disc or cylinder, however, which had to be playable on home machines, changed the picture completely.

Features that had to be standardized were:

1. Use of disc or cylinder
2. RPM of turntable
3. Pitch of grooves (number of grooves per inch)
4. Shape of grooves
5. Choice between lateral and vertical recording
6. The electrical recording "characteristic"

Most modern records are of the disc type, are made to revolve at 33⅓ rpm, are recorded at an average of 225 grooves per inch, and employ grooves which are shaped to receive a spherical-tip stylus in such a way that the contact is exclusively with the sides and not the bottom of the groove. Monaural recording is of the lateral type, and the recording characteristic is the RIAA curve.

Lateral and Vertical Recording

The recordings of Young, Scott de Martinville, and Cros were all lateral: the recording stylus moved from side to side in a plane approximately parallel to the record, and inscribed a visible wavy line, a graph of time *vs.* instantaneous stylus position.

The recordings of Edison, on the other hand, were vertical, or hill-and-dale. The vibrations of the recording stylus were in a plane perpendicular to the record, and the groove variations were in depth, up and down rather than from side to side.

These two methods of recording are illustrated in *Fig.* 4–1. Edison was the chief champion of hill-and-dale recording; he used the vertical method in his cylinders and, later, in his heavy discs. Vertical recording gave way entirely to lateral in the commercial home record, but remained fairly popular in broadcast studio use for a while. The death blow to monaural vertical recording was dealt by a classic article on the subject by Pierce and Hunt, which clearly showed that the level of inherent distortion in the record-reproduce process was much lower with the lateral method. The reader may note with satisfaction the power of the just pen.

The main advantage of lateral recording is that second harmonic "tracing" distortion (not to be confused with *tracking* distortion), is drastically reduced or eliminated. Tracing distortion is caused by the fact that the reproduc-

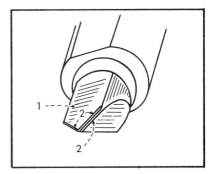

Fig. 4-2. Recording stylus. 1 — cutting face; 2 — burnishing facets.

ing spherical stylus tip is guided in an imperfect vibrational pattern, by groove walls that were cut by a differently shaped recording stylus. (See *Fig.* 4–2).

In the case of the laterally-cut groove the inaccurate component of the playback needle's vibrations are almost exclusively up and down. This spurious mechanical motion, however, is not necessarily translated into an electrical output signal from the pickup. If the pickup has little or no electrical response to vertical stylus motion (a characteristic possessed by modern high-quality monaural pickups, and called "low vertical response") then the distortion in motion is not allowed to influence the signal.

The channelling of spurious needle vibrations associated with tracing distortion into vertical motion is called pinch effect, and is illustrated in *Fig.* 4–3.

Stereo Disc Recording

Stereo, as we have seen, requires two independent recorded channels. The earliest of the stereo discs used a separate, laterally recorded groove for each of the channels; the outer half of the record was devoted to one channel, and the inner half to the other. Playback had to be through a dual-headed pickup.

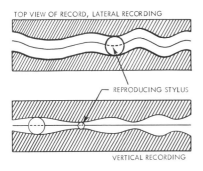

Fig. 4-1. Record groove in a vertical and in a lateral recording.

Recording Characteristics

A recording "characteristic" is the curve of frequency response, flat, sloped or otherwise, of the recording system; that is, it describes the frequency *vs.* amplitude characteristics of the recorded signal.

In the early days of recording the artist shouted into a horn, and as much of the recording diaphragm vibrations as could be preserved were applied to the wax. There was no problem of what to do with the bass, since so little bass was there in the first place.

There is a definite problem in recordings of wide frequency range, however, with regard to signals at both ends of the frequency spectrum. Both the bass and treble must be doctored in a specific pattern, and for reasons that will be discussed.

Bass Equalization

Below a certain frequency called the *turnover* frequency the bass portion of the recorded signal is progressively attenuated, at the rate of 6 db/octave. (This means that the signal voltage of the bass signal is halved with each lower octave). This is for the purpose of preventing the bass-modulated grooves from cutting over onto each other.

If the vibrations of the recording stylus are to represent equal energy over the frequency spectrum the stylus must have constant average velocity at all frequencies. A little thought will indicate the fact that constant average velocity does not mean constant excursion (distance of travel) at different signal frequencies. As a matter of fact the excursion must exactly double with each lower octave. If the stylus moves from side to side .01 inches at 500 cps, then to record a 250 cps signal at the same average velocity it must move .02 inches.

This is illustrated in *Fig.* 4–6. It may be seen that the average velocity of the stylus is determined by the distance through which it vibrates, divided by the time consumed. Since the time for one cycle of vibration at 250 cps is double that of the time for one cycle at 500 cps, the distance through which the needle vibrates would also be doubled in a constant-velocity device.

The continual increase of stylus excursion at lower frequencies creates difficulties. It places excessive demands on the recorder cutting head, and the recordist must space his grooves liberally to prevent the large groove deviations of heavy bass passages from overcutting into adjoining grooves. He must either sacrifice playing time by widely spaced grooves, or risk the severe distortion caused by groove cut-overs.

Fortunately there is a solution to the problem, made possible by the versatility of our playback equipment. It is to attenuate the bass at a specified, uniform rate, and to restore the lost bass in playback by equipment which progressively accentuates the lower frequencies, at the same rate and starting at the same turnover frequency. The "equalization" curve of the playback equipment—which is to

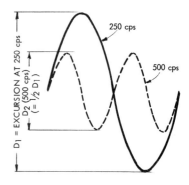

Fig. 4-6. Illustration of the increase of needle excursion at lower frequencies to maintain constant average velocity. At 250 cps the needle travels through only one vibration during the same time that two 500 cps vibrations are accomplished; the distance of travel at 250 cps must therefore be doubled.

say its frequency discrimination characteristic—will then be the reciprocal of the equalized pattern into which the recorded signal has been forced.

The final result is a return to the original signal characteristics as they existed before they were doctored, but it is achieved with smaller groove deviations in the bass range.

Treble Pre-emphasis

Special difficulties are also involved in recording the high-frequency portion of the signal spectrum. The surface noise that is produced in the course of the needle-record contact is spread quite evenly over the frequency spectrum in terms of *energy per cycle*. This means that each higher octave, containing twice the number of cycles, will have twice as much surface noise. Considering further the increased hearing sensitivity in the higher ranges, the common-sense conclusion must be that record surface noise is primarily a treble phenomenon. This means:

a) The "masking" effect of record surface noise will occur primarily in the treble range. Recorded sound at the higher frequencies will tend to get lost in the mud.

b) An attenuation of treble amplification in the playback equipment will severely reduce the surface noise relative to the total signal.

If the treble frequencies of the recorded program material are progressively emphasized or "boosted," a recorded signal will be created that will sound unnaturally shrill in playback. A reciprocal treble attenuation introduced in the playback chain will make the sound natural again. This record-reproduce procedure is just what is used in modern records, in order to improve the *signal-to-noise* ratio.

The initial progressive boosting of the high frequencies is called treble *pre-emphasis,* and the frequency at which the boost takes hold is called the

pre-emphasis *transition* frequency. *Fig.* 4–7 illustrates the change in surface noise, relative to the recorded signal, that the pre-emphasis technique brings about. Treble attenuation in playback simultaneously reduces surface noise and corrects the high-frequency level of the signal back to its original state.

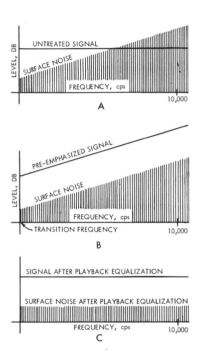

Fig. 4-7. Effect of treble pre-emphasis (B) and playback equalization (C) on the level of surface noise relative to the recorded signal.

Over-all Recording Characteristic

The over-all pattern of modern record equalization is illustrated in *Fig.* 4–8.

While the principles of bass and treble record equalization have been generally agreed upon for a long time, the best way to introduce such equalization—the turnover and treble transition frequencies, and the rates of attenuation or boost

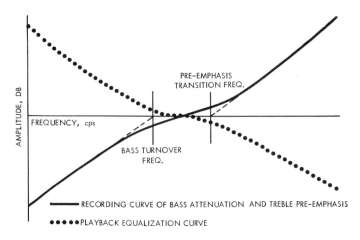

PRE-EMPHASIS
TRANSITION FREQ.

AMPLITUDE, DB

FREQUENCY, cps

BASS TURNOVER
FREQ.

——— RECORDING CURVE OF BASS ATTENUATION AND TREBLE PRE-EMPHASIS

● ● ● ● ● PLAYBACK EQUALIZATION CURVE

Fig. 4-8. Pattern of recording and playback equalization.

to employ—has been the subject of much disagreement. Recording equalization is a double-edged sword, and can itself cause difficulties. For example, too much treble pre-emphasis increases high-frequency distortion at the same time that it reduces noise, by unduly increasing the sharp, crowded groove excursions required at high frequencies.

General industry agreement on the RIAA equalization curve was reached in 1955-1956.

Dynamic Range in Recording

Dynamic range refers to the range of power, from pianissimo to fortissimo, that the reproducing equipment is capable of handling. For disc records it is the ratio of the amplitude of the heaviest recorded signal to the softest.

In a sound reproducing system the upper limit of the dynamic range would be determined by the power capability of the equipment, the lower limit by the noise level. On a disc the upper limit of the recorded dynamic range is determined by the allowable groove excursions, and the lower limit by the surface noise.

In the bass, groove excursions are re-stricted by the danger of cut-over, as discussed previously, even when there is attenuation below the turnover frequency. In the treble range the groove excursions do not become so great as to involve cutting over into adjacent grooves, but there is another danger, just as serious. The high-frequency groove "wiggles" are confined to short groove lengths, and the greater the excursions of the recording stylus the sharper the corners of the wiggles become. (The condition becomes increasingly aggravated as the inner record diameters are approached.) This tends to create a groove shape which cannot be followed faithfully by the reproducing needle, and results in increased distortion and record wear.

The technique of recording with treble pre-emphasis reduces the relative surface noise in the signal, and it would seem that treble pre-emphasis should increase the dynamic range of sound that can be recorded onto a disc. Unfortunately, however, while pre-emphasis does extend the lower limit of the dynamic range by reducing surface noise and allowing softer signals to become audible, it increases treble groove excur-

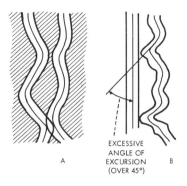

EXCESSIVE
ANGLE OF
A   EXCURSION   B
(OVER 45°)

Fig. 4-9. (A) Over-recorded grooves, showing cut-over. (B) Result of over-modulation, with excessive angle of excursion.

Fig. 4-10. Modern disc recorder — the Scully lathe.

sions at the same time, thus restricting the upper limit of dynamic range that can be used without distortion. It can be seen that the decision as to the optimum characteristics to use for recording is not a simple one.

Fig. 4—9 shows over-recorded grooves which have cut over onto each other, and grooves with excessively sharp corners.

Modern Techniques for Increasing Dynamic Range

Older records had a severely limited dynamic range. Not too many years ago recorded orchestral crescendos were considerably watered-down versions of the original, and any really soft passages would have been wasted, as they would have been drowned out by surface noise.

Modern records have increased this dynamic range, approaching that of the original sound, by the use of several techniques. First, the surface noise has been greatly reduced through the use of improved materials. This makes it possible for the recordist to cut soft musical passages at a very low level. It takes a much smaller groove wiggle to over-ride

the inherent irregularities of the material of the groove wall itself.

Second, there are methods for extending the upper limit of the dynamic range. One such method is to employ *variable-pitch* recording, that is, to increase the spacing between grooves automatically when a heavily recorded passage appears. Another method is to attenuate instantaneously only those dangerous portions of the signal which might create cutover or high-frequency distortion. The use of improved pickups and needles, making it possible to trace heavily recorded grooves more faithfully, also works to increase the allowable dynamic range.

Recording Equipment

The recording turntables, cutting heads, amplifying equipment, and tape machines (the latter make the initial recording) must be of the highest quality, so that a minimum of limitation is put on the capabilities of the reproducing equipment. While a detailed discussion of recording equipment is not appropriate here, a professional recording turntable and cutter is illustrated in *Fig.* 4—10.

5.

PICKUPS AND NEEDLES

THE MODERN PICKUP, unlike the older "sound box" of the acoustical phonograph, is an electrical generator driven mechanically by the vibrations of the stylus. The pickup's output appears as an alternating voltage between two terminals; the extent to which this voltage faithfully represents the recorded signal is the degree of fidelity of the pickup.

Modern pickups that are in general use belong to one of two basic categories, with one exception. These two categories are the piezo-electric and the magnetic (there are variations within each); the exception is the capacitive pickup.

Magnetic pickups are by far the most common in high-quality installations. They may in turn be classified into three types: the variable reluctance pickup, the moving-coil pickup, and the moving magnet pickup.

These differences relate to the method of conversion of mechanical energy into electrical energy. The methods of electrical generation are the same for either monaural or stereo pickups; the simpler monaural pickups will be discussed first, and it will then be seen that the same types of electrical generators can be used in a two-channel configuration.

The Variable Reluctance Pickup

In order to understand how the variable reluctance pickup works we must first briefly consider some of the fundamentals of electro-magnetic theory.

A magnetic "structure" refers to a system which includes a magnet with north and south poles, and a magnetic path between the poles, in which magnetic forces exist. The structure is often referred to as a magnetic *circuit*, analogous to an electrical circuit in many ways. The magnet itself is like the electrical generator, and the magnetic path is like the load connected to the generator.

In an electrical circuit the amount of current flow (within the power capability of the generator) is determined by the generator voltage and the circuit resistance. For a given voltage, the lower the resistance the greater the current flow.

In a magnetic circuit the "flux" of

the magnetic field in the path between north and south poles is determined by the strength of the magnet and by the *reluctance* of the magnetic path (analogous to *resistance* in electrical terminology).

Different materials have different reluctances. For example, air has a high reluctance, iron a low one. For the same magnet, then, a relatively strong magnetic field will exist if the path between magnetic poles is of iron, and a relatively weak one if the path is of air. Intermediate values will be associated with a path which is partly iron and partly air.

We need to discuss one more phenomenon before completing the theoretical background of the variable reluctance pickup. If a coil is moved with its conductors perpendicular to a magnetic field (as in an electrical generator) a voltage appears at the coil terminals. The appearance of this voltage. is due to the *relative* change between coil and magnetic field, and it doesn't make any difference which of the two does the changing. The same effect will be created if the coil remains motionless, and the magnetic field changes intensity.

The design of the variable reluctance pickup is based upon the above phenomena. *Fig.* 5-1 shows a simplified diagram of a coil and magnet in a pickup. There are two magnetic paths; each consists of half of the U-shaped iron, the iron shank of the stylus, and the air in the gap on either side of the

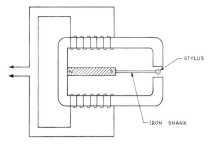

Fig. 5-1. Simplified diagram of the variable reluctance pickup.

stylus tip. The reluctance of the magnetic path on one side will be at a minimum when the stylus is closest to the iron on that side, since the smallest part of the magnetic path will be air.

As the needle is displaced from side to side by the record groove, the reluctance of each magnetic path is continuously changed. The magnetic field will also be changing, and the varying field across the conductors of each coil causes a varying voltage to appear at the output terminals. The coils are connected together in such a way as to add their signal voltage, but to cancel hum. The arrangement is similar to the push-pull design discussed in Chapter 9.

It will be seen that the only work that the needle must do is to move its small mass in and out of the gap and to change the field. It does not have to exert any considerable force on the voltage-generating element, as it did in older pickups. This is an advantage from the point of view of reduced record wear, low distortion, and smooth frequency response.

Another characteristic of variable reluctance pickups is low voltage output (low, at any rate, compared to the piezoelectric type). A typical monaural reluctance pickup, for example, is rated as having 10 millivolts output at a given reference standard of groove modulation.

A further characteristic of variable reluctance pickups is that the output voltage is proportional to stylus *velocity*, not to the distance of needle travel. We have seen that the recorded signal is doctored before it is cut into the disc. A pickup whose output is proportional to needle velocity will present us with the doctored signal, not the original one. Therefore variable reluctance pickups must always work in conjuction with a preamplifier stage, which increases the signal voltage and, at the same time, compensates for the frequency equalization existing in the recording.

The Moving-Coil Pickup

The moving-coil pickup works in an inverse manner to the variable reluctance unit. It has a coil, and the output voltage appears at the coil terminals, but in this case the magnetic path is fixed and the coil itself is the moving element.

Such a coil must, of course, be very light and small. There is no room for many turns of wire, and the output voltage is low even when compared to that of a variable reluctance pickup.

The moving-coil pickup, like the variable reluctance type, requires a preamplifier to boost its voltage and to compensate for recording characteristics. (The moving-coil output is also velocity-dependent.) The low output voltage calls for high amplification in the preamplifier, and the problems of hum pickup are proportionately increased.

The Moving-Magnet Pickup

The moving-magnet pickup works on the same principle as the moving-coil pickup, but the relative positions of the magnet and of the coil are reversed. As in the case of the variable reluctance pickup, the coil of the moving-magnet pickup is stationary. The moving element is a tiny permanent magnet which forms part of the shank of the needle.

Advances in the techniques of producing magnetic material have made it possible to use the moving-magnet principle. A very small magnet can now be made with a field sufficiently strong and resistant to de-magnetization.

Piezo-Electric Pickups

The piezo-electric or "crystal" pickups generate their voltages in an entirely different manner from the magnetic units. Certain crystalline materials, such as Rochelle salt and barium titanate ceramics, have the property of producing voltages at their surfaces when they are bent or twisted. The stylus is harnessed to slabs of these materials, and the modulations of the groove apply either a twisting or bending force to the slabs.

The output voltage appearing at the cartridge terminals is much greater than that produced by magnetic pickups, and may be from ½ volt to as high as 4 volts. Furthermore the crystal pickup does not produce a voltage proportional to the stylus velocity, but to the amplitude of the stylus movement. The frequency characteristic of the output, however, is approximately the reciprocal of the typical recording characteristic used in modern records. Therefore the output of the crystal pickup is fed directly to the amplifier, without the use of a preamplifier. Both the voltage amplification and the equalization of the preamplifier would play havoc with the crystal pickup's output.

Crystal pickups are sometimes designed with a particular recording characteristic in mind (the advent of the standard RIAA characteristic makes this much more practical). The crystal pickup has the advantages of significantly greater simplicity in installation, freedom from hum, and reduced cost.

Older crystal pickups had disadvantages which have been overcome to a large extent. Rochelle salt is subject to deterioration from heat and humidity, but the ceramics are not. The stiff mechanical system of the older units has given way to needle systems which move relatively easily.

Crystal pickups may also be designed for the type of operation that was previously associated with magnetic pickups only. The value of electrical resistance across the pickup influences its performance. When a low value of resistance is placed across the crystal pickup it takes on the flat, unequalized performance characteristics of the magnetic pickup. Output is also severely reduced, although it tends to be greater than that of the magnetic unit.

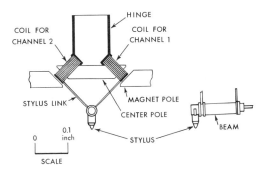

Fig. 5-2. Basic working parts of a stereo moving-coil pickup. The coil for each channel can move individually and generate its own signal voltage. (After Westrex)

Stereo Pickups

Stereo pickups employ the same kinds of electrical generating devices listed above, with the difference that a stereo pickup must have two generating mechanisms driven by the single needle. Each of the electrical generators in *Fig.* 5–2 responds only to the diagonal components of needle motion, at forty-five degrees left of vertical for generator No. 1, and at forty-five degrees right of vertical for generator No. 2. If the needle is made to vibrate at forty-five degrees left, only generator No. 1 will produce electrical output representing the vibration. If the needle is made to vibrate at forty-five degrees right, only generator No. 2 will produce output. For all other needle motion each generator will pick off its respective diagonal component, and will produce an output voltage representing one channel of the recorded stereo signal.

There is always some interaction between the two generators, but it can be kept sufficiently low. The amount of interaction, described by the term *separation*, is usually plotted over the frequency spectrum and rated in db. A separation of 20 db at a particular frequency, for example, means that the signal voltage inadvertently picked up by the wrong channel is 20 db less

than the correctly sensed signal. 20 db represents a voltage ratio of ten to one; ten percent of the right channel will appear in the left channel output. This would not significantly compromise the stereo effect.

The diagram of *Fig.* 5–2 represents a moving coil stereo pickup. Moving-magnet, variable reluctance, and ceramic generating systems are also used for stereo. The output of these cartridges is lower than that of their monaural counterparts; of the order of a few millivolts for the magnetic units, and 8 to 10 millivolts for the ceramic cartridge when the latter is used loaded for unequalized output.

Electrical Connection of the Pickup

Pickups are normally connected to the input of the amplifier or preamplifier with low-capacitance shielded cable. The "termination" of the pickup refers to the value of resistance that the amplifier input places across this cable, and is very significant in the case of both variable reluctance and crystal pickups.

Manufacturers' recommendations are usually the best guide to use when it is possible to adjust the value of resistance across the pickup (some preamplifiers allow for this), but a few general principles may be stated here:

1. With a magnetic pickup, too low a shunt resistance will attenuate the high frequencies; too high a resistance may allow an excessive peak in the upper treble. Typical values of resistance for reluctance pickups range from 22,000 to 56,000 ohms.

2. With a crystal pickup, too low a shunt resistance will attenuate the bass; too high a resistance will over-emphasize the low frequencies and create a peak in the upper bass. Typical values of resistance for crystal cartridges are 470,000 ohms to 3.0 megs., when the pickup is to be used as pre-equalized, high-output unit. When the pickup is designed for unequalized low-output applications (in which case it can be substituted directly for a magnetic pickup, without any circuit changes) the typical value of shunt resistance is 47,000 ohms.

Needles

The type of contact established between the needle or stylus and the record groove is illustrated in *Fig.* 5–3. It will be seen that the spherical tip of the stylus does not touch the bottom of the groove.

It is obvious that the stylus tip should be of such material that it maintains its shape in spite of repeated use. It is also important that the tip have a smooth, unmarred surface. Sapphire fulfills these conditions for a relatively short time,

diamond for a much longer period. Estimates of the life of a sapphire stylus in a high quality system are rarely above twenty-five hours of playing time, while diamonds are normally good for more than a thousand. *Figure* 5–4 illustrates the relative wear of diamond, sapphire and osmium.

Although diamond needles may be, initially, as much as ten times as expensive as sapphire, one of their outstanding characteristics, at least in a high-quality installation, is economy. More important is the freedom from the danger of periodic degradation in reproduction quality and in record wear.

Vertical Force on the Pickup

The *vertical stylus force* on the pickup (rated in grams) is the force required to keep the needle in firm contact with the groove walls at all times. This is sometimes called "tracking pressure," but the latter is an improper term because units of pressure are in terms of force per unit area. The higher the vertical force the greater will be the erosion of the groove walls, but this does not mean that it is possible to arbitrarily decrease the weight on a given pickup. Only pickups with very high compliance, whose needles can be displaced with very little force, can afford to work under conditions of low stylus force.

Typical vertical stylus forces required by modern high-quality pickups range from one to four grams for stereo units, and six to eight grams for monaural units. When the force is reduced below its optimum value distortion, often severe, results. Therefore it is better to err in the direction of a little too much than a bit too little. Pickup arms normally allow the user to adjust the vertical force, by the use of an adjustable counterweight or by an adjustable retaining spring. The manufacturer's specifications should always be consulted carefully, but it must be remembered that the specified stylus force may be for an optimum installation, and lower

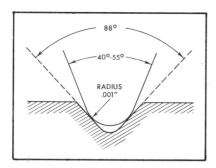

Fig. 5-3. A 1-mil stylus tip in the record groove.

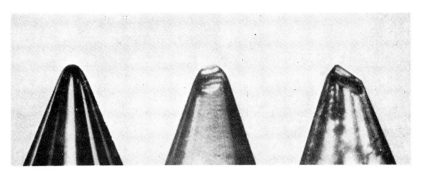

Fig. 5-4. Three microgroove (one mil) needles that have been subjected to the same amount of wear. Left to right: diamond, sapphire, and osmium. (Courtesy The Tetrad Company, Inc.)

quality tone arms may require somewhat higher forces. The way to really know when the stylus force is right is to note the point at which distortion is reduced to an acceptable value. This is difficult to do without instruments.

Pickups exhibit a resonant peak in output at the top of their frequency range. This peak, which is caused by "plastic resonance," is not really created in the pickup itself, but results from the interaction between the mass of the stylus and the compliance of the record material. At the high frequencies involved the mechanical suspension of the stylus no longer has any appreciable effect on stylus motion, and the record groove walls no longer act as though they were made of a rigid material. It is as though the needle were traveling in the groove as a free body, stretching

the record material as it presses against it. This mass-elasticity system must, of course, have a natural resonant frequency, determined by the compliance of the record material and the mass of the needle.

It is desirable to have this resonant frequency as high as possible so that it does not interfere in the usable audio range, and it is also desirable to damp the resonant peak. To this end the needle is made as light as possible, and the needle suspension employs some sort of damping material. Although the stiffness of the needle suspension is reduced to an insignificant value at high frequencies, the resistive or friction component of this suspension remains the same at all frequencies, and the amount of damping is not changed at high frequencies.

6.

PICKUP ARMS

A good tone arm should do the following:

1. Present the pickup to the record in a position tangent to the groove being played, or as close to this ideal as possible.
2. Keep maximum stability in the face of external mechanical shock, or warped and/or off-center records.
3. Keep "warp-wow" to a minimum.

Tracking Error

A rigid pickup arm which is pivoted at one point cannot keep the pickup parallel to all grooves. The divergence from tangency is called *tracking error*, and it results primarily in increased distortion, due to the fact that the vibration axis of the pickup is held obliquely to the groove that drives it.

It is possible, however, to keep the pickup within a few degrees of tangency at all points by mounting a fairly long arm, of bent shape, in a special way. The arm is mounted so that the needle would "overhang" the turntable spindle if it were swept past, as illustrated in Fig. 6–1. Such a mounting position, when calibrated properly to the length of the arm, keeps the cartridge-groove angle almost constant, although the absolute angle between groove and pickup with this arm mounting would be far from correct with a straight arm. The cartridge is therefore mounted in the arm at an "offset" angle, to bring it back to tangency. The exact amount of overhang depends both on the length of the arm and on the offset angle.

It will be seen from the foregoing that the offset angle of a bent pickup arm does not correct for tracking error in itself. The most critical element is the amount of overhang, and this should be correct to at least .03 inch. A bent arm incorrectly mounted can be much worse than a straight arm correctly mounted.

The correct mounting position for a pickup arm relative to the record spindle is usually furnished by the manufacturer, often by means of a template, and this should be followed with painstaking care.

Arm devices for carrying the pickup cartridge across the record so that it

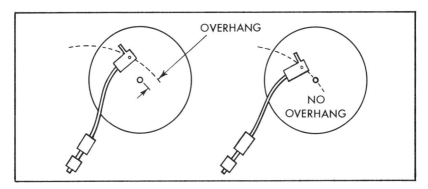

Fig. 6-1. Correct mounting position of an offset tone arm, showing overhang. The incorrect mounting at the right results in higher tracking error than would exist with a straight arm.

remains tangent to the record groove at all points have been devised. One such device is an overhead track which substitutes for a radial pivot; another such device is a multi-pivoted parallelogram structure which corrects the angle of the pickup as it moves across the record.

These devices introduce new problems of their own. The simplest (and at the same time entirely adequate) solution to the tracking problem appears to be the use of a single-pivot arm of sufficient length — nine inches pivot-to-needle distance is common — designed with the correct offset angle and installed for the correct overhang. While such an arm does not reduce tracking distortion to zero, the amount of distortion introduced is small enough to have very little significance in relation to the other distortions associated with the record playing mechanism.

Tracking distortion is a function of the tracking error divided by the groove radius. This is to say that the same tracking error will produce twice as much distortion at a 3-in. radius groove as at a 6-in. radius groove. The correct design of the arm must be in terms of the lowest tracking error distortion rather than the lowest tracking error. A properly designed arm will therefore

show somewhat higher values of absolute tracking error in degrees than one which is designed merely for minimum tracking error.

Tone Arm Balance

There are three kinds of static balance — unstable, stable, and neutral. There is also dynamic balance, which has little significance for tone arms and which will be discussed later.

Unstable balance occurs when the line between the centers of gravity of two sides of a balanced system passes above the pivot, as in (A) of *Fig. 6–2*. If either side is tipped it will continue to move. This is undesirable for tone arms, because it means that the vertical stylus force is not the same in all arm positions, and will vary with warped records. It is easier for the needle to leave the groove when it hits a bump.

Stable balance, useful in scales, occurs when the line between centers of gravity passes below the pivot, as in (B) of *Fig. 6–2*. In this case there is a tendency for the system to return to the horizontal if it is tipped. The stylus force of a tone arm in stable balance is again different for different arm positions. Like the unstable arm a warped record will create instantaneous changes in stylus force, although in the opposite direction.

41

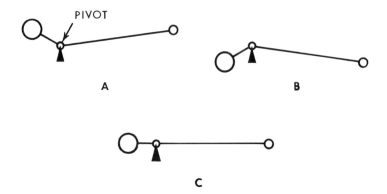

Fig. 6-2. Three kinds of static balance — (A) unstable, (B) stable, (C) neutral.

When an arm in stable balance is lifted by an uneven record surface stylus force will increase, creating a tendency for the needle to dig into the record.

Neutral balance, most desirable for tone arms, is illustrated in *Fig. 6–2(C)*. Here the line between centers of gravity passes through the pivot. The system will be in equilibrium at any angle, and stylus force does not vary with vertical motion of the arm.

Neutral balance for the horizontal plane can be provided in various ways, but the principle is the same; the line between centers of gravity of the forward and rear sections of the arm must pass through the pivot for horizontal motion. Five different methods of keeping the horizontal pivot on this line are currently employed (see *Fig. 6–3*):

a. The counterweight and cartridge shell are connected by a straight arm, which must then enter the offset cartridge shell obliquely.

b. The counterweight and cartridge shell are in line as in (*a*), but in order to allow the arm to enter the shell at a right angle the arm is given a double curve.

c. A single-curve arm enters the cartridge shell at a right angle, and the center of gravity of the counter-

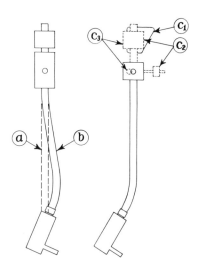

Fig. 6-3. Five methods currently employed for maintaining horizontal neutral balance. Letters are referred to in the text.

weight is shifted in the opposite direction, either through the shape of the counterweight, by an additional adjustable side weight, or by moving the horizontal pivot in from the vertical pivot.

It is no more expensive to design an arm with neutral balance than one which does not have it. There is an allied problem, however, which affects the form of this design—vertical warp-wow.

Vertical Warp-Wow

All records must be considered as having normal warp which creates vertical arm motion. Even a record that fulfills NAB Standards of good engineering practice is allowed a 1/16-in. vertical warp, and obviously all records do not, particularly after use, meet this standard.

When the cartridge moves up and down along an arc the needle must move back and forth along the groove, as illustrated in *Fig.* 6—4. This means that the instantaneous relative speed between needle and groove will be changed. It makes no difference, of course, whether the platen has actually been slowed up or the needle moved along the groove;

the audible and measured wow is the same.

It can be seen from *Fig.* 6—4 that there will be minimum longitudinal needle motion when the pivot controlling vertical motion is as far back as possible, and when the height of this pivot brings it as close to the plane of the record surface as possible (more precisely, to the average plane of the warped surface).

A warped record tends to exhibit more vertical motion when it is supported at its center than when it rests on its outer surface. It is therefore a good idea to have a slightly raised outer section for the record mat.

Dynamic Balance

The term "dynamic balance" has been widely and incorrectly used in relation to tone arms. This is a standard term in physics, and refers to balance as it is affected by the momentum of the different parts of a balanced system when this system is set into rotation. A statically balanced system may, when set into rotation, set up centrifugal forces on each side which are not in line with each other. In the case of rotating ma-

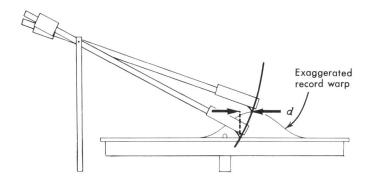

Fig. 6-4. Illustration of vertical warp-wow. When the arm is lifted by a warped record the needle moves a distance d along the groove, reducing relative needle-groove velocity.

chinery this can produce trouble at the pivot. In the case of tone arms, however, the magnitude of such forces is at the most of the order of thousandths of a gram, and it has no significance for tone arm operation.

Counterbalance: Spring vs. Weight

There are three methods currently used for providing stylus force: a) the use of a spring to cancel out all but the desired mass of the cartridge and arm, with no counterweight; b) the use of balanced masses, with a spring applying the desired stylus force; and c) the use of an underbalanced counterweight to provide stylus force.

There is a rationale to each of these methods. The counterweightless, all-spring system provides the lowest inertia, but the greatest sensitivity to external mechanical shock and to tilt of the turntable because of the extreme imbalance of masses. The balanced mass, spring-loaded system provides the greatest stability under conditions of imperfect leveling and exposure to external mechanical stimuli. The underbalanced counterweight system is simplest, and

the one least liable to go out of adjustment. It can be used without sacrifice of performance quality compared to the spring-loaded arm, if the mounting of the entire turntable-arm system provides sufficient isolation from external mechanical shock and is self-leveling.

Tone Arm Mass

When the tone arm is set into motion vertically by record warp, or horizontally by record eccentricity, inertia becomes a controlling element. The greater the inertia at the end of the arm the more the stylus will alternately dig into the groove and try to leave it.

This inertia must not be confused with stylus force, even when the stylus force is provided by unbalancing the counterweight. In order to set the arm into motion the inertia of *both* front and rear sections must be overcome. The momentum of both cartridge and counterweight is in opposition to the required reversal of arm motion when record warp changes slope, or when an eccentric center hole swings the arm back and forth. The arm should therefore be as light as possible consistent with rigidity.

7.

AMPLIFIERS

A COMMON-SENSE DEFINITION of the word "amplifier" is "a device that makes things bigger." But in technical language the term has a much more restricted meaning; the device referred to becomes an amplifier only when the things that are made bigger consist of energy-patterns. The nature of amplification can probably be better understood by considering first the operation of another energy transmission device that is *not* an amplifier—an instrument that is called, in mechanics, a machine.

The machine receives input power, shapes it for the required task, and releases it, less the inevitable losses from friction, in its new form. Were it not for these losses the amount of energy released would be exactly equal to that received. Although the Indian hunter was able to bring down buffalo with bow and arrow, his arrow was driven by less energy than had been put into flexing the bow. His machine was able to store and concentrate the power that it received when the string was drawn back, so that the shaft sped with lethal velocity. Without the machine the hunter's

strength would have been totally ineffective.

The mechanical lever, the acoustical horn, and the electrical transformer are other examples of transmission devices whose useful output energy, while re-formed in such a way as to be most suitable for the application at hand, must always be somewhat less than the input energy. The word "machine" applies to mechanical devices only; the term which includes all instruments of this nature, whatever type of energy is transmitted, is *passive transducer* (from *traducere*, to lead across).

An amplifier is also an energy transmission device, and hence a transducer, but it is an active one. It does that which would be impossible without a sort of engineering sleight-of-hand—it provides a transmission channel whose output, seemingly the same in identity to the received stimulus, contains more energy than its input. The difference is that between a pulley and a powered capstan. It is obvious that the useful output energy of an amplifier cannot be greater than the total energy supplied, any more than it is possible for such a condition to exist in the case of a passive transducer, or energy will have been created out of nothing. The trick is that the input stimulus borrows and directs power from an independent second source (such as the electric company's generators), and shapes this independent power to its own form.

The need for amplifiers arises when we are dealing with impulses which must remain in a very definite time pattern if they are to be useful. One of the earliest amplifying devices was the pipe organ, whose player was able to control, with relatively light pressures of his fingers, the steady flow of air produced by sweating bellows-operators. Amplifiers in the more generally accepted sense, however, were invented when nineteenth century technology became concerned with the transmission and reproduction of vibratory power: first sound, and then radio waves.

Sound consists of successive and alternating compressions and rarefactions radiated by an oscillating source. The telephone and the phonograph therefore depended for their operation on acoustical, mechanical, or electrical forces which continually reversed their direction, and which carried the transmitted intelligence in the time sequence and pattern of their oscillations. The

problem that faced engineers was to extend telephonic communication over longer distances, to make phonograph reproduction louder than was possible with the original, limited power.

The first approach, successful up to a point, was to increase the efficiency of the passive transducer elements. But the best acoustical and electrical passive transducers that could be designed to harness effectively the sources of this oscillatory energy proved inadequate. Sound generators like the human voice mechanism, or the phonograph pickup diaphragm following the record groove, simply didn't have enough driving power for the work they were called upon to perform, even with the carefully designed horns that increased their radiating efficiency. The solution was to inject outside energy into the systems and to use the original stimulus as a controlling rather than a driving force, which is to say, to amplify.

Early Amplifiers

In 1876 Edison patented a device which he called an *aerophone*. It was a pneumatic public-address amplifier, illustrated in *Fig. 7–1*, in which the speaker's voice controlled the instantaneous flow of compressed air by means of a sound-actuated valve. The air was thus released in vibratory bursts and

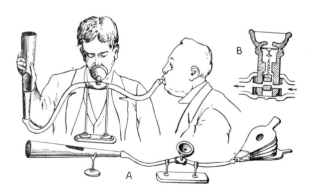

Fig. 7-1. (A) Edison's aerophone, or pneumatic amplifier, provided a sound transmission channel into which additional energy was injected in the form of compressed air. Inset (B) shows how the sound-actuated valve throttled a steady flow of air, to create an instantaneous variation in flow that imitated the original sound vibrations.

puffs similiar to those that came from the speaker's mouth, except that they were more powerful, and the speech, still intelligible, was louder. Edison envisioned broadcasting in stentorian tones over distances of several miles. Such a system has actually been used in ports, but it found its main application in the designs of two British inventors who applied it to the phonograph. Short developed, and Parsons further improved the *auxetophone*, whose pneumatic valve was attached directly to a phonograph reproducing stylus. Although pneumatic phonographs produced a constant background hissing noise due to escaping air, they were fairly popular in Europe, and in the early nineteen hundreds the French Pathé company experimented with them with a view towards developing talking motion pictures. (See *Fig.* 7–2.)

Another type of device, the mechanical or friction amplifier, found more favor in the United States. It was used in certain models of Columbia's cylinder "graphophone," as shown in *Fig.* 7–3. The reproducing stylus of these

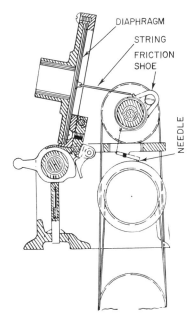

Fig. 7-3. The stylus of Columbia's cylinder graphophone was coupled to the reproducing diaphragm through a string and a friction shoe that picked up extra energy from the rotating drum.

instruments, instead of being coupled directly to its diaphragm as in standard acoustical phonographs, was attached to the diaphragm via a string and friction shoe that passed over a rotating drum. When the stylus tightened up on the string, friction between the shoe and the drum was increased, and force picked up from the drum augmented the displacement of the diaphragm. When the record groove forced the stylus in the opposite direction, so as to loosen up on the string, the diaphragm returned to its original position due to spring tension. In this way the vibratory path of the diaphragm was extended by the energy of the independently driven drum, and sound output was increased.

Both of the above designs were referred to at the time as relay systems.

Fig. 7-2. French Pathé phonograph of 1905, with compressed-air amplifier.

The original stimulus was thought of as touching off latent power, like a relay runner passing the baton to his successor. These systems were the forerunners of our present-day electronic amplifiers, but they were themselves doomed to a short life. The golden age of mechanics, when the diabolical iron fingers that set printing type, tabulated sums, and rolled cigarettes were the wonders of applied science, was passing. Electronics was taking over, and the amplification of sound was destined to include an intermediary step, the temporary transformation of mechanical vibratory energy into electrical energy possessing the same characteristics in time.

The Vacuum-Tube

The device which really opened up the field of amplification was the vacuum-tube. Fleming had made an electronic valve that contained two electrodes sealed in an evacuated glass chamber, a cathode emitter and an anode collector. When the cathode was heated a cloud of electrons was given off, and if the device was then connected in series with a battery, in such a way that the anode was positively charged relative to the cathode, the electrons were attracted to and entered the anode. Since electrons in motion constitute electrical current the circuit was completed through this one-way path.

The stream of electrons flowing in the empty space between cathode and anode provided an especially favorable area for sensitive control of the current drawn from the battery. The opportunity was seized by De Forest, who introduced a control element into the valve by inserting a "grid"—an open network of fine wire—across the electronic stream. De Forest's grid was a sieve mechanically, but if it was charged negatively relative to the cathode, it tended to repel electrons (which are also negatively charged) and to retard current flow. A weak input "signal" voltage applied between grid and cathode, varying according to a given frequency and wave form, produced an imitative variation in the relatively heavy output current flow, as may be seen in *Fig.* 7–4. This output power could follow the input characteristics more closely than had been possible with any other device designed previously. The limits imposed by mechanical systems—their intractability when subjected to forced vibration in modes foreign to their natural resonances, the uneven restraint of elastic suspensions, and the fact that supposedly rigid parts become flexible when subjected to vibration at high frequencies—all disappeared, and development workers found themselves operating in a dream-world of virtually massless units, where incredibly swift oscillation could be controlled and amplified without having to reckon the price of inertia, elasticity or gravity.

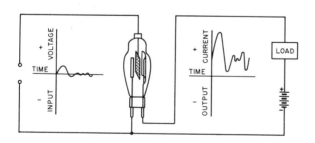

Fig. 7-4. Amplification of a weak electrical impulse is achieved by a vacuum-tube circuit. The input electrical stimulus has alternating polarity, while the output is in the form of pulsating one-way current.

48

An early application of vacuum-tube amplifiers was to the generators and receivers of radio waves. Like sound, electromagnetic radio energy is oscillatory, although at frequencies which may be millions of times higher than those of acoustical vibrations. The element analogous to the phonograph horn is the antenna, acting as a passive transducer to space—and, as in the case of the horn, efficient antennas were not enough. With transmitter output amplified, however, from a few watts to hundreds of kilowatts, and receiver sensitivity raised to the point where a few millionths of a volt at the antenna created usable reception, wireless global communication became possible. Other applications followed quickly. The recording and reproduction of sound, the detection and measurement of very small quantities of light, sound, pressure, or voltage, the myriad tasks performed by calculating machines, and the sensitive control and regulation of massive machinery became electronic functions.

But with poetic injustice, after the vacuum-tube has served as the vehicle for the modern science of electronics, it is being prepared for the scrap-heap, at least in certain applications. The vacuum-tube has several disadvantages, foremost among which is its unreliability. Besides having too short a normal life, the possibility of failure at any time after installation must always be taken into consideration by design engineers. The unreliability of the vacuum-tube is such an accepted fact-of-life that instead of being wired permanently into the circuit, like other components of electronic apparatus, it is plugged into a tube socket to facilitate periodic replacement. In addition to this unreliability the vacuum-tube requires a separate power supply to heat its filament (diverting and wasting most of the energy taken from the independent source), it must be given a warm-up period prior to service, and it is too bulky in some applica-tions. The feature which redeems all of these disadvantages is the superb control which may be exerted over the captive electron steam.

Without abandoning the last feature, new ways in which electrons can be made to submit to instantaneous regulation at high frequencies are being investigated. The transistor, a revolutionary experimental device a few years ago, can be ordered by the part number at radio dealers, and development work is also being performed on magnetic, dielectric, and other types of amplifiers.

Transistors

From the electrical point of view materials may be classified according to their resistance to the passage of current, as conductors, insulators, and semi-conductors. In an atom of a good electrical conductor the outermost electronic shell is held so loosely that its electron inhabitants are not associated exclusively with any particular parent atom. The attachment, originally weak because of the relative distance from the nucleus, disappears with the close atomic spacing typical of these materials, and the outer electrons are free to rove. These *free* electrons are able to respond to the force of an electric potential applied across the conductor, and form an electronic wind blowing across the relatively stationary atoms themselves towards the positive terminal, constituting the flow of current. Current does not flow to any appreciable extent in non-conductors because the atoms of insulators hold on grimly to their outer shell electrons, which are more numerous, closer to the nucleus and much more difficult to dislodge.

To impart motion to an electron is to give it added kinetic energy. Quantum requirements dictate that the electrons must fill certain discrete energy levels, that is, that they cannot possess a random amount of energy, and that each energy level can only accommodate a given number of electrons. Therefore the energy of an electron can only be increased or decreased by an amount which brings it into a new step level in which a vacancy exists. The quantum levels of the atoms of a conductor have vacancies, permitting electronic transfer from one level to another. The energy levels of the atoms of insulators, on the other hand, are all filled, so that the system is locked.

The energy level states of semi-conductors (substances such as germanium, selenium, silicon, and the oxides of copper and barium) form a special case. The locked system is upset by the presence of minute impurities, whose outer electronic orbits contain electrons in a number either greater than or less than the amount normal to the pure substance, and which introduce energy levels capable of releasing or accepting electrons. Where the number of outer electrons is greater than normal, excess electrons are available for current flow in the form of an electronic wind, and the substance is called a donor. Where the number of outer electrons is less than normal, the substance is called an acceptor, and vacancies are available for electronic current flow in the form of "hole" conduction (an effective migration of the unfilled spot from one atom to another, a phenomenon which has been aptly compared to the motion of an air bubble in water). These two modes of conduction occur in opposite directions and are called, respectively, *n-type* for negative, and *p-type* for positive. Hole conduction has a positive designation because the migration of holes has the same experimental effect as the transfer of positive charges.

The development of semi-conductor devices has followed the same course as that of the vacuum-tube, from two-terminal systems providing a one-way electronic path, to three-terminal systems in which the electronic flow is made subject to control from an area astride the path. Semi-conductors were used as rectifiers of alternating current long before the word transistor was coined. A potential applied in one direction across the junction of a *p*-type and an *n*-type substance will encounter relatively low resistance to current flow, but relatively high resistance if the polarity and hence the direction of current flow is reversed. This is because the electrons and holes travel towards each other for one polarity, facilitating transfer across the junction, and away from each other for the opposite polarity. The rectifying action may also be described from the point of view of energy-level states; for one polarity, electrons belonging to energy levels capable of releasing electrons are driven towards atoms containing energy levels capable of receiving added electrons, while for the other polarity the opposite effect occurs.

A *p*-type substance sandwiched between the two *n*-type substances, or vice-versa, creates the basic design of one type of transistor amplifier. The conducting properties of one of the junctions for "wrong-way" current may be controlled by creating either hole or electron carriers in the sandwiched element (by means of a current through the other junction)—to put it another way, by causing a shift in the electron energy level states responsible for conduction: The pattern of variation of a small controlling current shapes the instantaneous resistance of the unit, and large currents may then be forced to follow the same pattern in time.

The transistor requires no warm up period, is smaller (see *Fig.* 7–5), cheaper in operating cost, and is potentially so much more reliable than the vacuum-tube that it may be wired permanently into the circuit rather than plugged into a socket. Transistor hearing aids, for example, are smaller than their vacuum-tube counterparts, consume only a small fraction of electrical power for

50

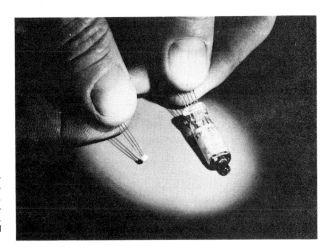

the same amplification (they have no A battery) and may ultimately be expected to require less service. The transistor has been developed to a point where it can duplicate many, although not all, of the vacuum-tube functions.

Magnetic Amplifiers

The electrical amplifiers that have been here described provide circuit paths whose resistance to current flow is varied by an input signal. Such a path may also be produced by an electro-magnetic rather than a resistive unit, which is called a *saturable reactor*.

The impedance of an electrical coil to alternating current is far more than would be expected from the inherent resistance of the wire. Each time that the current increases, drops to zero, and then increases in the opposite direction a magnetic field around the coil builds up, collapses, and builds up again with reversed polarity. This pulsating magnetic field cuts the wires transversely each time that it builds up and each time that it collapses, inducing current of such instantaneous direction as to oppose and reduce the original flow. This is the descriptive analysis of inductive reactance. In the magnetic am-

plifier the input signal controls the intensity to which the self-induced field can build up, and hence it controls the electrical impedance of the coil.

Among the factors that determine the intensity of the field are the number of turns in the coil, the size of the core, and the material of the core. None of these can be manipulated at high frequencies, but there is another, more easily controllable characteristic that can influence the coil's field strength and a.c. impedance—the magnetic condition of the core. The core will not continue to accept added magnetization indefinitely; there is a natural limit to its capabilities. As the current is increased the core begins to *saturate*, which means that a further increase of current flow through the coil will produce less than the corresponding increase in magnetic field strength. The degree of this saturation may be controlled, electrically, by the input signal.

A separate winding on the same core, through which the controlling input current flows, will cause the degree of saturation to increase and decrease according to the instantaneous polarity and value of the input signal. A larger current flowing in the output winding,

51

drawn from an a.c. source of power, will then vary in step with the varying impedance.

In practice it is found necessary for the independent energy source of the magnetic amplifier to supply pulsating direct current rather than alternating current, as shown in *Fig. 7–6*, so that the saturation effect of the current in the output winding can never oppose that of the input winding. Pure direct current in the output circuit, however, such as is used with vacuum-tubes and transistors, will not work. Direct current would remain uninfluenced by the changes in core saturation; the impedance of the coil to d.c. is entirely a matter of the resistance of the wire conductor. Thus the power that is varied by the input signal is itself a steadily oscillating quantity, but it is a relatively simple matter to separate and extract the amplified impulses from the alternations of the power source. For this purpose the frequency assigned to the power supply is made much higher than the highest-frequency input that is to be amplified.

Magnetic amplifiers are very reliable, have the ability to withstand severe shock, and require no warm-up period. They are also exceptionally efficient, because most of the impedance which they introduce into the output circuit is of a type called reactive, which does not itself absorb energy. Magnetic amplifiers are at present advantageously applied in circuits which must control appreciable amounts of power at relatively low frequencies—adjustable-speed motors, winding reels, automatic pilots, voltage and frequency regulators, and other automatic control apparatus. A magnetic amplifier used in servo work is illustrated in *Fig. 7–7*.

Functional Categories of Amplifiers

In the beginnings of radio an experimenter was able to buy a single type of "audion" or three-element vacuum-tube. Today the number of specialized tube types that have been designed for particular jobs runs into the thousands. Amplifiers may, nevertheless, be classified into a few basic functional categories. These concern (1) the amount of output power required, (2) the band and band-width of frequencies covered, and (3) the degree of wave form distortion to the original stimulus that can be tolerated.

Heavy tasks, such as the radiation of sound into a room, the engraving of the undulated groove in a disc record, the control of machinery, or the radiation of radio waves by a transmitting antenna, require "power" amplifiers, so-called because of the relatively large amounts of power regimented to the appointed duty. "Voltage" amplifiers or amplifying stages do not differ in principle. They, too, increase the input power, but they are used where the primary requirement is to raise the signal voltage (without a corresponding decrease in current) and where the amount of output power needed is not very great. These conditions are normally present, for example, when the output of a stage of amplification is used to drive another amplifier, perhaps a power amplifier insensitive to weak signals, or when the output is connected to a final load with

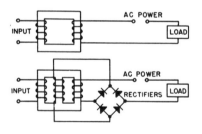

Fig. 7-6. The top diagram shows the essentials of a magnetic amplifier circuit. Current in the input winding controls magnetic saturation of the core, which in turn controls the impedance of the output winding to the flow of alternating current. The bottom diagram includes rectification of the a.c. power to pulsating d.c.

Fig. 7-7. "Servo" magnetic amplifier used to drive a mechanical positioning system. (Courtesy Magnetic Amplifiers, Inc.)

modest power requirements, such as a pair of earphones.

Amplifiers are designed for various frequency ranges between zero cycles (direct current) and the microwave band. The upper limit of the latter is considered to be about 100,000 megacycles, approaching the infra-red region of the electro-magnetic spectrum. Microwave amplifiers are used in radar and television-relay stations. An amplifier that can build up d.c. stimuli, or stimuli that change only slowly, is required for various types of measurement, including such medical applications as the detection of minute body potentials. Each frequency region has its own problems of amplifier design, with regard both to the amplifying units themselves and to circuitry. Microwave circuits, for example, use hollow-pipe wave guides instead of connecting wires, and the transmission lines are often referred to as plumbing because of their physical appearance. Special tubes for microwave oscillators and amplifiers—magnetrons, klystrons, and traveling-wave tubes—have been designed.

Most amplifiers cover only a small portion of the electrical frequency spectrum, but certain types of signal embrace an unusually wide band of frequencies. Video signals, for example, which represent variations of dark and light across successive strips of the picture screen, cover the range from thirty cycles to four megacycles, a ratio of better than 100,000 to 1. Amplifier stages for such signals require special design treatment. A sacrifice in gain must be made in order to achieve broad-band operation.

The degree of output inaccuracy in a high-quality audio amplifier is ordinarily less than the degree of hearing discrimination for such inaccuracy. The main sources of distortion in sound reproducing systems are the electro-mechanical and electro-acoustic transducers —pickups and loudspeakers—but even here amplification helps matters. When the efficiency requirements of the passive transducers are reduced by virtue of the amplifier it is easier to subdue annoying mechanical resonances, a step that improves performance considerably.

The possibilities of securing amplification from new types of devices have by no means been exhausted, nor have current amplifying devices been fully covered here. Research in basic amplifier units and in applied circuitry is continually going on.

8.

PREAMPLIFIERS AND CONTROL UNITS

THE SIMPLEST ELECTRICAL phonograph system is one in which a very high output pickup is connected directly to the grid of a power amplifier tube. Crystal pickups with outputs of 3 or 4 volts, for example, have been used to drive the grid of an output tube designed to operate with relatively small input voltages, without intermediary voltage amplifiers.

Normally, however, the output of the pickup, whatever the type, is fed to a voltage amplifier called a preamplifier.

Special Tasks of the Preamplifier

The first job of the preamplifier is to amplify the pickup voltage, without distortion. The preamplifier works with very small signals. Any stray noise or hum induced in the pickup, the pickup lead, the circuit components, or the tubes themselves may compete with the signal itself in magnitude, at least to the extent of providing an annoying noise background.

We have seen that FM broadcast standards for signal-to-noise ratio require that the noise be at least 60 db down from the signal, that is, that it be no more than one-millionth of the power of the signal. When the signal itself is of the order of a small fraction of a microwatt the power of stray hum and noise in the circuit must be kept low indeed in order not to intrude.

One special quality of good preamplifiers, therefore, is that they have very low noise and hum. Power amplifiers with signal-to-noise ratios of 80 db (100 million to one) or better are not too unusual, but we must lower our standards for phonograph preamplifiers, especially when using very low output pickups.

The next job of the preamplifier is to introduce the correct frequency discrimination to compensate for the bass attenuation and treble boost in the recorded signal—to *equalize* the output of the magnetic pickup.

The frequency response of the phonograph section of a preamplifier is described by the curve of its equalization. The excellence of preamplifiers in this respect is indicated by the accuracy with which they adhere to the correct equalization curve. It is obvious that describing the frequency response of a preamplifier in terms of frequency extremes —20 to 20,000 cps, for example—would tell us nothing useful about the performance characteristics of the unit. What we want to know is whether the frequency response of the preamplifier is within, let us say, one db of the proper equalization at all points of the curve.

When the desired frequency response curve of a particular audio component happens to be flat (as in the case of a velocity pickup, power amplifier, or loudspeaker) it is unfortunate that the meaning of the phrase "frequency response" sometimes departs suddenly, and a meaningless recitation of frequency limits takes its place. But it is no less true here than in the case of the equalized circuit, that a meaningful description of frequency response must tell us how accurately the output conforms to the ideal at every point of the curve, whatever the shape of the ideal curve.

Frequency Discriminating Circuits

Frequency discriminating circuits—equalizers for preamplifiers, or variable tone controls—may be of the feedback or direct type, but in either case the basic circuit element is the *voltage divider*.

A resistive voltage divider is illustrated in *Fig.* 8—1. If the series resistor is 9,000 ohms and the shunt resistor is 1,000 ohms, as shown, the output voltage of the network will be just one-tenth of the input voltage, or 20 db down. Since resistors do not change their value with frequency, the same attenuation will exist at all frequencies. The frequency response of this resistive circuit is plotted in the graph of *Fig.* 8—1; it can be seen that the "curve" for output voltage has not changed from the curve for input voltage, except that it is reduced in amplitude by a factor of ten.

Now consider the circuit of *Fig.* 8—2, in which the lower arm of the divider has had a capacitor added in series. At very high frequencies the *reactance* of the capacitor (analogous to a.c. resistance) is negligible—the capacitor acts as though it were shorted out. The attenuation of the circuit at these frequencies will therefore be substantially the same as in *Fig.* 8—1—by the full factor of ten, or twenty db.

As the frequency is lowered the reactance of the capacitor will increase. It will begin to affect appreciably the impedance of the lower arm of the voltage

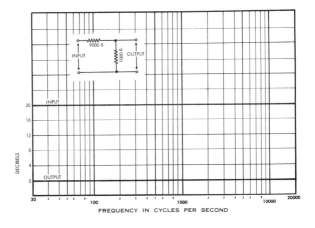

Fig. 8-1. Resistive voltage divider. The input is attenuated by a factor of ten (a 10 to 1 voltage ratio is 20 db), but there is no frequency discrimination.

divider, and the ratio of the two arms; thus it will also affect the amount of attenuation.

At some lower frequency the reactance of the capacitor will be equal to 1,000 ohms, the value of the resistor in the lower arm. This is taken to be the point at which the frequency discriminating characteristics of the circuit take hold (although it can be seen that the change is gradual), and is called the *transition frequency.* In the case of the circuit under discussion it is the frequency at which bass boost is considered to begin.

As the frequency is lowered further the total impedance of the voltage divider's lower arm increases more rapidly. The attenuation of the circuit is decreased progressively until finally, at very low frequencies, the voltage divider lets through practically all of the input voltage, as illustrated in the graph of *Fig.* 8–2.

We call such a circuit a "bass boost" network, but obviously we have really boosted nothing. What we have actually done is attenuated a whole band of frequencies, and then selectively let a part of the attenuated frequency spectrum back in.

The same circuit configuration as that of *Fig.* 8–2 may also be used for treble attenuation, by choosing the circuit values so as to shift the entire curve to the right (upwards in frequency). A treble boost or bass attenuating network, on the other hand, must work in an inverse manner. Application of the same sort of analysis as above to the circuit of *Fig.* 8–3 will show the reader why the circuit of *Fig.* 8–3 can be used for treble boost or bass attenuation.

Tone Controls

The fixed equalizers which have been discussed can be used to compensate for known frequency curves built into the record. There are also many conditions affecting frequency response which are not known beforehand by the circuit designer. These include room acoustics (discussed in more detail in a later chapter), deficiencies in associated equipment which may unduly boost or attenuate portions of the frequency spectrum, changes in overall volume which change our bass hearing sensitivity, and variations in program material caused by differences in microphoning, studio or hall acoustics, and so forth.

We cannot hope to compensate accurately for all such conditions, but flexible tone controls, intelligently designed

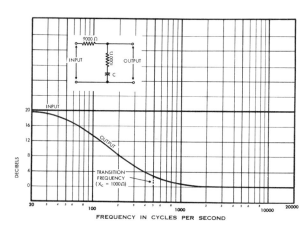

Fig. 8-2. Resistor-capacitor voltage divider, and resulting bass boost.

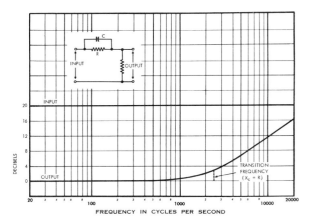

Fig. 8-3. Treble boost circuit

to approximately correct for conditions typically encountered, can help a lot. These tone controls work on the same principle as the frequency discriminating voltage dividers discussed previously, with the difference that the rate of boost and cut, or the transition frequencies, or both, are controllable.

Fig. 8–4 illustrates a treble tone control, and the equivalent circuits for

maximum treble-boost (slider at the top of the potentiometer) and maximum treble-cut positions (slider at the bottom of the potentiometer). *Fig.* 8–5 illustrates a bass tone control, also with equivalent circuits for maximum bass boost and maximum bass cut.

The effectiveness of a tone control is determined by the extent to which it affords accurate compensation for varying conditions. It has been the writer's experience that this object is best served

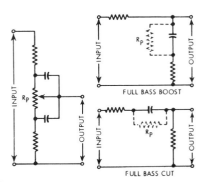

Fig. 8-4. Continuously variable treble tone control, with equivalent circuits for maximum boost and cut shown at the right. Elements which are substantially out of the circuit, due to the insertion of Rp in series with the capacitor, are shown in dotted line.

Fig. 8-5. Continuously variable bass tone control. Equivalent circuits for maximum boost and cut are shown, with significant elements at these positions shown in heavy line.

57

by tone controls with either varying transition frequencies, or with transition frequencies which are some distance from the audio spectrum mid-point, perhaps 500 cps for the bass and 3,000 cps for the treble. In any case the way *not* to judge the "effectiveness" of a tone control circuit is to twist the knobs all the way in each direction and to see how unnaturally screechy and boomy the sound can be made. Tone controls which really work where they are needed, without unduly affecting the mid-range, usually have a less dramatic but far more musical effect, even in their extreme positions.

Loudness Control

We have seen, in discussing the Fletcher-Munson effect, that as the overall volume of sound is decreased our bass hearing sensitivity is reduced significantly. In listening at volume levels lower than that of the original music, then, the original tonal balance will be changed, and it is desirable to be able to introduce compensatory bass boost. Some people like to do this themselves, with the bass control; others like to have it done automatically, by a bass boost circuit tied to the volume control. In the latter case the volume control becomes a "loudness" control.

Control units performing the functions of preamplification and control of bass, treble, volume, and record equalization are available commercially as separate units, and also in combination with the tuner, the power amplifier, or even the record player. There is really no inherent advantage of one scheme over another, except for operating convenience, if the design is properly executed. Placing the control elements near power transformers or phonograph motors increases the hum problem, but this does not imply that the more difficult solution will be any less satisfactory.

9.

POWER AMPLIFIERS

Strictly speaking, the term "power amplifier" refers to the output stage of an amplifier. This stage receives signals of relatively high voltage but negligible power, and releases signals of the same wave form but of sufficiently high power to drive a loudspeaker. In its less restricted meaning, however, the term is used to represent the entire group of stages (other than preamplifier and control stages) which are housed on the power amplifier chassis. The chassis usually includes a general-purpose voltage amplifier or amplifiers, a phase splitter, and the output stage itself, plus a "power supply" for all of these stages.

A detailed description of the functioning of different audio circuits is not considered to be within the scope of this work. Rather it is intended to provide a general understanding of the function and working of the stages listed above.

Voltage Amplifiers

A typical commercial power amplifier (the term used in the free sense as described above) is designed to produce its rated power output at an input signal of one-quarter to one-half volt. But the output stage proper needs a much higher signal voltage at its grids to be driven to its rated output. Most output pentodes, under their usual conditions of operation, require signal voltages in the range between 15 and 25 volts for full power output, and a triode such as the 6B4 requires as much as 70 volts. The amplifier must thus provide the facility for amplifying the relatively weak input voltage, a facility called *voltage gain*. With an input signal of ¼ volt, and the requirement that a driving signal of 20 volts be applied to the output stage grids, a voltage gain of 80 must be available.

A limited amount of voltage gain can be secured from a step-up transformer, but it is impractical to use transformers for large amounts of voltage gain; this gain must be provided by one or more vacuum-tube stages in the amplifier. The difference between voltage and power gain should be clearly understood: the amount of voltage gain in or preceding the power amplifier has no bearing on its

current changes in the vacuum-tube, and let us further consider that the condition of no distortion is represented by a back-and-forth motion in which the saw is pushed forward from its neutral position (operating point) exactly the same distance as it is pulled backward from this position.

It would be conceivable that, for one reason or another, the operator of the saw cannot push as hard as he can pull, and that while he pulls the saw back a foot the best he can do on the push, with the same maximum effort, is half a foot. We will use this condition to represent the fact that the tube current flow can follow the direction of the input voltage on the increase, but is unable to do so in the negative direction due to cut-off characteristics of the tube.

We now introduce a handle at the other end of the saw, and a second woodsman (subject to the same limitations on the force of his push relative to that of his pull), who pushes when our first sawyer pulls, and vice versa. What will happen? Each motion of the saw is subject to two unequal forces, a pull from one direction and a lesser push from the other, but the *sum* of these two forces will be the same for each direction of motion. The saw must then move the

same distance coming and going. It is being operated in push-pull.

In the case of our tubes, the total output current during each half of the cycle is made up of two parts, one full (corresponding to maximum current flow in one tube) and one incomplete (corresponding to operation of the other tube past the cut-off region), as illustrated in *Fig.* 9–4. An analysis of the operation of a push-pull stage will show that, with perfect balance between the two halves, the part of the distortion that is eliminated is that represented by spurious *even* harmonics only. It is possible to take advantage of this fact by choosing the operating point of the tubes to produce very low odd harmonic distortion, at the expense of allowing higher even harmonic distortion, and then to cancel out spurious even-order harmonics by push-pull circuitry.

The forces of the sawyers were, from the point of view of time, applied out of phase one with the other. But these forces were also applied to the saw out of phase from the point of view of direction. There were thus two phase reversals, and the forces combined to create a final power equal to the sum of the separate parts. Similarly, each of the tubes in push-pull are driven out-

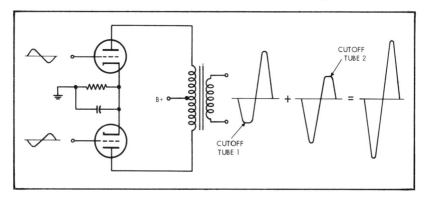

Fig. 9-4. Push-pull operation. The input signal is divided in two; each half is amplified by a tube which is operating past cut-off, but the out-of-phase outputs are reassembled into a single undistorted signal.

of-phase, and their individual outputs are out-of-phase from the point of view of time. The two output currents are combined in such a way, however (as shown in *Fig.* 9–5) that the direction of flow in the output transformer constitutes a second phase reversal, and the final output power is equal to the sum of the powers available from each tube.

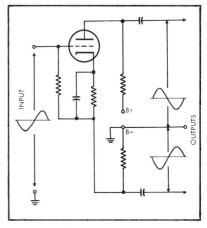

Fig. 9-6. Split-load phase-splitter stage.

ground, are thus out of phase with each other as required.

Negative Feedback

The application of negative feedback in amplifier circuitry, as an additional method of reducing distortion, is so important that a separate chapter is devoted to the subject.

Source Impedance of the Amplifier

Amplifier output terminals are labelled according to the speaker impedance to which they are meant to be connected: 4 ohms, 8 ohms, 16 ohms, etc. A mismatch downwards (from an 8-ohm tap, for example, to a 4-ohm speaker) will usually not affect quality appreciably but will reduce the power capacity of the amplifier—how much depends on the amplifier itself. A mismatch upwards, however, from a lower-impedance tap to a higher-impedance speaker, can usually be used with impunity. The fact is that the amplifier is "mismatched" to the speaker in an upward direction, in any case, over most of the frequency spectrum. We will see that the rated or nominal impedance of the dynamic speaker holds over only a small frequency band, usually in the 150-400 cps

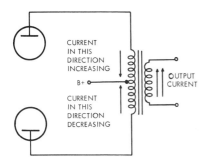

Fig. 9-5. How the out-of-phase halves of a push-pull circuit are combined in-phase.

Push-pull circuitry is universal in modern high-fidelity audio amplifiers. It can be used for both voltage and power amplifier stages: it is common in the former and universal in the latter.

The Phase-Splitter

Push-pull stages must be driven by two signal voltages which are identical except for phase—one must be in its positive half of the cycle at the same time that the other is in its negative half. There are various ways of splitting the signal in this manner, and the stage which does the job is called the *phase-splitter.*

One type of phase-splitter, called a *split-load* stage, is illustrated in *Fig.* 9–6. It will be seen that the currents through the two load resistors are in opposite directions relative to ground. The output voltages across these resistors, taken in each case relative to region, and that the actual speaker impedance increases manyfold at the frequency extremes.

The *source impedance* or *internal resistance* of the output stage (which is the source impedance of the amplifier) is an entirely different thing, although it is sometimes confused with the ratings of the output taps. The two terms used above are synonymous, and refer to the resistance that the speaker "sees," looking back at the amplifier, rather than to the load that the amplifier is designed to see.

The source resistance is effectively in series between the amplifier and the speaker, as the internal resistance of any generator is in series between it and the load. If the value of this source resistance is high, relative to the nominal impedance of the speaker, it effectively controls the relative voltage fed to the speaker at different frequencies. When the speaker impedance is high, as at the extreme frequencies, a maximum of voltage will be fed to it. This tends to create a combination of boominess and shrillness. Such used to be the case, as a matter of fact, in the old pentode power amplifier without negative feedback, and this was the main reason for the generally acknowledged superiority of triodes in the output stage prior to the general use of feedback.

The source resistance has another significance relative to amplifier performance. If the speaker is set into vibration, especially at some low frequency near the natural resonance of its mechanical system, it will tend to continue to vibrate after the signal has stopped (an action referred to as *hangover*). Such a tendency is common to any mass-elasticity system that has received a mechanical stimulus.

The tendency to hangover in speakers is controlled by damping, of which there are three kinds: mechanical, acoustical, and magnetic or electrical. The last of these is a function of the source resistance. When the speaker voice-coil undergoes vibrations it acts as an electrical generator, and the vibrations are braked electrically by the source resistance. Electrical energy created by motion of the voice coil is dissipated in the source resistance, which the speaker generator sees as a load, and vibrations unauthorized by the signal are brought to an abrupt halt.

The source resistance of an amplifier, relative to the speaker impedance, is also expressed as a ratio called the *damping factor*. A high damping factor represents a low relative value of source resistance.

The Power Supply

The amplifier requires certain operating voltages—tube filament supply (normally *a.c.*), plate and screen voltages (*d.c.*), and in some cases fixed grid voltages (*d.c.*). These are provided by the power supply, which steps the power company's voltage up or down as the case may require, and rectifies and filters the input *a.c.* (converts it to a smooth *d.c.*). This power supply should be hum-free, rugged, and stable. The voltage should not change when large current demands are made by the signal, or distortion will be increased.

10.

NEGATIVE FEEDBACK

L ET US SUPPOSE that the power steering system of an automobile is
somewhat out of adjustment, in that it
over-responds when pulled to the right.
The driver senses the trouble instantaneously, and compensates for the
defect by applying less force on right
turns. This is negative feedback in
operation, although it is not automatic;
the feedback "circuit" includes the
driver himself.

The function of an audio amplifier, as
of a power steering system, is to control
large amounts of power by small
amounts of power. The electrical signal
from a radio tuner or phonograph pickup cartridge, representing the broadcast
or recorded sound, may have enough
power to drive a pair of earphones but
is hopelessly inadequate for a loudspeaker. Before the electrical currents
can be reconverted to sound of appreciable volume they must be *amplified,*
that is, their power must be increased.
At the same time there must be negligible distortion—the fidelity of electrical
representation must not be changed.

The electron tubes that are the heart
of the amplification process perform
with good, but not perfect fidelity. Prior
to the universal acceptance of negative
feedback as essential to high-fidelity
amplification, "undistorted" amplifier
power meant maximum output at which
the harmonic distortion was no greater
than 5 per cent. One-twentieth of the
output signal could consist of spurious
harmonics not present in the original
input. Modern engineering techniques
have been able to reduce this distortion
figure by a factor of 100 (leaving pickups and loudspeakers far behind), and
the most powerful of such techniques is
the application of negative feedback.

Feedback In Amplifiers

A common explanation of how negative feedback reduces amplifier distortion goes something like this: part of the
output signal is fed back into the amplifier out of phase, thereby partially
cancelling distortion products. Such an
explanation is not incorrect, but it is
incomplete.

If no mention is made of the point
at which the feedback signal is intro-

duced in relation to the point or points at which the distortion is generated, the above explanation becomes a house of cards that can be .easily demolished. It is only necessary to point out that the out-of-phase feedback signal can reduce the amplitude of the faithful part of the signal in exactly the same amount as it reduces the distortion elements, thus leaving the distortion percentage unchanged. Clearly we must dig a little deeper. We will see that if the negative feedback signal is introduced into the amplifier at a point *before* the distortion is generated, it acts as a pre-compensating element which reduces the percentage of distortion in the output signal.

Consider the case of a pure sine wave applied to an imperfect amplifier. The output signal fed to the loudspeaker will be a distorted version of the input, as illustrated in *Fig.* 10–1. It is evident that a characteristic of this amplifier is the reproduction of positive peaks with insufficient relative amplitude.

If the entire process took place very slowly we could compensate the signal input for such a characteristic and produce a pure sine wave in the output. As the signal approached its positive peak we could turn up the level control of the signal generator to just the right position at each moment (monitoring the amplifier output with an oscilloscope) so that the extra signal voltage would force the instantaneous amplifier output to conform to the sine-wave pattern. The erratic output characteristic of the ampli-

fier would then be corrected for at every point by an inverse characteristic of the signal input from the generator. This would be a nonautomatic feedback system, in which the differences between output and original input signals are sensed by the operator, and the corrections applied manually.

The periods of time involved in the amplification of an audio half-cycle, of course, are very small, and correction for amplification characteristics through feedback must be applied automatically and without measurable time delay. The negative feedback circuit does just that; it compares the distorted output signal with the undistorted input, and applies to the amplifier a corrective signal corresponding to the differences between the two.

Automatic Correction

Fig. 10–2 illustrates the automatic correction applied by negative feedback. The steps illustrated in sequence show the transmission of the signal through the amplifier and back through the feedback circuit; the time taken by each step is so small that it cannot be measured by ordinary methods, and the process may be considered instantaneous.

The distorted amplification of a sine wave is illustrated in (A) of *Fig.* 10–2. Part of the distorted signal is tapped from the amplifier output and fed back to the input in such a way that the phase is exactly opposite, as illustrated in (B). Notice that the feedback signal is fed

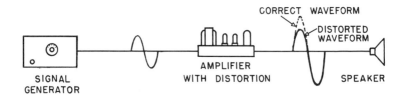

CORRECT WAVEFORM

DISTORTED WAVEFORM

AMPLIFIER WITH DISTORTION

SPEAKER

SIGNAL GENERATOR

Fig. 10-1. Distorted reproduction of a sine-wave signal. The instantaneous amplification is reduced on positive peaks.

back to a point before that at which the distortion was generated, so that the distorted signal is mixed out of phase with an undistorted signal.

Two things must happen. The original input signal will be reduced in strength, and a corrective enlargement of the first half-cycle will appear in its wave form. It is as though the circuit knows what the amplifier is going to do to the signal's positive peak and sends in the signal forewarned and forearmed. Where the defective amplifier will not furnish enough gain, at the positive signal peak, the signal itself is pre-compensated by having too much voltage relative to the negative half-cycle. The output signal shown in (B) of *Fig.* 10–2 is reduced in power but has a lower percentage of distortion.

It is important to know that while gain is sacrificed by negative feedback, amplifier *power capability* is not. The third step in the feedback process is illustrated in (C) of *Fig.* 10–2. The corrected input signal is increased to bring it back to its value before the application of feedback, and the original output power is restored at lower distortion. It is necessary, however, to drive the amplifier harder, that is, to provide a higher input signal.

Amount of Feedback

The amount of feedback, in decibels, is the ratio of the original signal voltage to the corrected signal voltage; thus the number of db of feedback also refers to the reduction of amplifier gain.

For example, suppose that a 30-watt amplifier is driven to full output by an input signal of .025 volt prior to the application of negative feedback. Twenty db of feedback (a healthy amount for an audio amplifier) means that the amplifier gain has been reduced to one-tenth of its former value, and 0.25 volt input will now be required to produce the same 30 watts. If the feedback is applied in such a way as to be fully effective the distortion and noise will also be reduced by a factor of 10.

Limitations of Feedback

Negative feedback seems to work wonders, but it is not magical, and it does not work against all types of distortion. It is completely wrong to design an audio amplifier carelessly and to assume that feedback will take care of any trouble. An amplifier circuit should be as "clean" as possible before feedback is introduced.

One limitation of feedback will appear obvious if we consider again the original example of the automobile power steering mechanism. If the trouble consisted of the fact that the front wheels of the car would not turn far enough, due to a bent frame acting as a mechanical stop, no amount of increased force used by the driver would help. Similarly, if the output wave form of an amplifier is clipped because the tubes have reached saturation and cannot pass more current, or have reached current

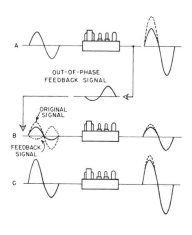

Fig. 10-2. How negative feedback corrects for distortion. Solid lines show actual signal.

cutoff, no change of amplifier gain, automatic or otherwise, can change the instantaneous value of the current being passed. Feedback can only help in those situations where an instantaneous variation in gain will produce a change in output.

Another limitation of negative feedback is inherent in the amplifier components themselves. The feedback circuit is designed to apply its corrective signal 180 deg. out-of-phase, but this phase relationship just does not hold up at the extreme low and high frequencies, especially when the output transformer is within the feedback "loop." The phase shift that occurs at the frequency extremes can be so great that the feedback becomes positive, in which case amplifier gain and distortion are increased or the circuit begins to oscillate.

Too much feedback used over a circuit whose phase shift is too high results in low-frequency "motor-boating" (the name given to oscillations of subsonic frequency because of their characteristic sound), or high-frequency squeals. Some of the worst effects occur when the oscillations break out only on signal peaks, producing distortion. The effect of high-frequency oscillation often imitates speaker rattle to perfection.

The successful use of large amounts of feedback is thus only possible with amplifiers which are of high quality to begin with. However, the application of moderate amounts of feedback can produce dramatic changes in low-cost circuits.

Fig. 10–3 illustrates a typical "voltage" feedback circuit. Part of the voltage across the output transformer's voice-coil winding is applied to the cathode resistor of an earlier stage. This has the same effect as applying the signal directly to the grid, but provides the additional convenience of a low-impedance path.

Feedback Equalization

A tone-control or equalizer circuit provides a transmission path whose gain changes for signals of different frequencies. A particular part of the frequency spectrum can thus be boosted or attenuated.

Negative feedback can be used to create such a discriminatory signal path. We have seen that the first action of negative feedback is to reduce circuit gain; if this action is made to vary with frequency we have a tone-control or equalizing circuit.

Fig. 10–4 illustrates the use of nega-

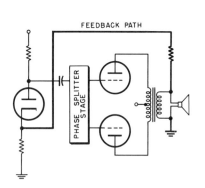

Fig. 10-3. Typical negative feedback circuit.

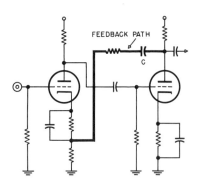

Fig. 10-4. Phonograph preamplifier equalization (bass boost) with negative feedback. The amount of feedback is progressively reduced below a selected transition frequency.

tive voltage feedback in a phonograph preamplifier, providing bass boost to compensate for the bass-cut characteristic in records. At higher frequencies the capacitor C is effectively a short circuit, but as the frequency is lowered the impedance of C rises, progressively reducing the feedback voltage applied to the cathode resistor, and hence increasing the amplification of the circuit. The circuit constants can be designed for the particular equalization curve required.

Feedback equalizer circuits possess anti-noise and anti-distortion characteristics over those portions of the frequency spectrum where the feedback is operative.

11.

LOUDSPEAKERS

THE SUBJECT OF LOUDSPEAKERS is so closely associated with that of enclosures that the two must be studied as interdependent parts of the same system. The division used here, which assigns separate chapters to each, is arbitrary and purely for the sake of convenience.

However, whatever type of enclosure is being used, the speaker must move its diaphragm according to the characteristics of the sound being reproduced. We will consider this problem first, ignoring the enclosure for the moment: later we will see that the demands made on the speaker mechanism itself vary according to the type of enclosure.

Until very recently there was only one type of loudspeaker in general use, the dynamic or moving-coil speaker. (The term *dynamic speaker* is sometimes mistakenly used to describe a speaker whose magnetic field is supplied by an electromagnet instead of a permanent magnet). The distinguishing feature of the moving-coil speaker is that the input electrical signal is applied to a coil which is "immersed" in a magnetic field, and

which is free to move back and forth along its axis. This *voice coil*, and its associated cone or diaphragm, then vibrates at the dictates of the signal, creating sound. To use the precise, almost archaic language of patent attorneys, the voice coil "executes excursions in the presence of a magnetic field."

The dynamic loudspeaker has reigned supreme for over twenty-five years; the first serious challenge has appeared only recently, in the modern version of the electrostatic speaker.

Basic Construction of the Dynamic Speaker

Fig. 11–1 shows the working parts of a dynamic speaker.

The input signal, of relatively low voltage, high current and high power, is applied to the stationary terminals. The current is then carried to the voice coil through flexible *pig-tail* leads, which make a solid electrical connection but a very compliant mechanical one.

When current flows through a coil a magnetic field forms around the coil, that is, the coil becomes a magnet with

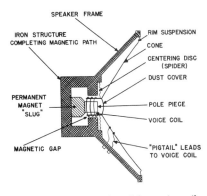

Fig. 11-1. Basic construction of the moving-coil loudspeaker.

north and south poles. If alternating current flows in the coil the instantaneous strength and polarity of the magnetic field must also alternate, according to the characteristics of the electrical current. In this case, of course, the current is alternating in the same manner as the mechanical vibrations of the original source of sound being reproduced.

The voice coil will therefore have a varying magnetic field about it. Now it is positioned in such a way that it is constantly immersed in the fixed magnetic field of the speaker magnet, whose polarity always remains the same. For one direction of voice-coil current the two fields interact in such a way that the voice coil is thrust forward: for the opposite direction of current, during the second half of the signal cycle, the coil is thrust backward. Alternating electrical energy is thus converted to vibratory mechanical energy.

The fixed magnetic field of most modern speakers is produced by a permanent magnet (PM) in the form of a ring, bar, or other shape. The magnet pictured in *Fig.* 11–1 is of the bar or "slug" type.

Such a bar of magnetic material will form a field about itself like that shown in *Fig.* 11–2, where the arrows indicate the direction that a test north pole (so-

called because it points towards the earth's north pole when free to do so) would tend to move. This field configuration could be plotted experimentally with a small magnetic compass.

It may be seen that the field is disposed evenly, and that it is diffuse rather than concentrated. We are interested in using *all* of this field, and over a rather limited space. Fortunately there is a simple method of concentrating the magnetic lines of force as we please.

Different materials have different reluctances in relation to magnetic fields, just as they have different electrical resistances. When an electrical circuit presents more than one path to a generator, most of the current will flow through the path of lower resistance; when materials of different reluctances present parallel paths to a magnet, most of the lines of force will be concentrated in the material of lower

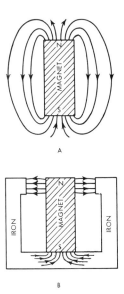

Fig. 11-2. (A) Magnetic field around a bar magnet, in air. (B) Magnetic field directed by a low reluctance path of iron.

71

reluctance. In the case of the magnet in (B) of *Fig.* 11–2 the choice of path is between the U-shaped piece of iron and the air surrounding the magnet. The magnetic lines of force, it can readily be seen, are concentrated in the iron.

But there is one point in the magnetic "circuit" at which there is no choice— there is nothing but air at the gap. And the gap is the business end of our magnetic structure. Virtually all of the magnetic lines of force must cross where we have arranged for them to do so, and where we have placed our voice coil. The voice coil thus receives the benefit of virtually all of the lines of force of the magnetic field.

The Mechanical System of the Speaker

The mechanical system of the loudspeaker is easily recognizable as a mass-elasticity system. This must be so unless we find a massless cone, or a suspension with infinite compliance or "give" in the axial direction and yet high stiffness in the radial direction. (The voice coil must be kept centered in the gap, even during violent motion, without rubbing.)

Since the speaker's mechanical system comes under the mass-elasticity category it must have a resonant frequency. A discussion of the effect of the speaker's resonant frequency on performance is not possible without taking into consideration the speaker enclosure—for one thing the enclosure may change this resonant frequency by more than an octave. If we assume that we are speaking of the resonant frequency of the speaker as mounted, however, we may come to certain conclusions:

1. Bass response falls off rapidly (at least 12 db per octave) below the resonant frequency. In a bass-reflex enclosure there are two resonant points: response falls off below the second.

2. Unless the speaker system is properly damped it will show a response peak at or somewhat above the resonant frequency or frequencies, and

the speaker will have poor bass transient response. The sound will be "boomy."

Speaker Damping

If the speaker is properly damped its output, other things being equal, will be flat over the resonance range until it begins to drop off, and transient response will be good. If the speaker is over-damped the transient response will be good but the bass will be attenuated, and may be significantly down from reference level at resonance. The term *damping* has a very specific meaning, as pointed out in our first chapter: it is the introduction of a resistive element (friction, or its equivalent) into the speaker's mechanical system in three distinct ways, all of which, however, have the same effect.

1. Mechanical resistance in the suspensions themselves—literally friction— which is normally minor.

2. Acoustical resistance contributed by the enclosure, and that associated with the work actually performed in radiating sound.

3. An equivalent mechanical resistance created by the speaker's electromechanical system. This system acts like a generator, and is loaded down by the source resistance of the amplifier. (An intuitive understanding of this effect can be achieved by taking a loudspeaker with a heavy magnet, and gently working the cone back and forth while the speaker is not connected to anything. Then short out the speaker terminals one to the other, or connect the speaker to an operating amplifier with a high damping factor, and again try to work the cone back and forth. It will feel as though the voice coil is being retarded by some heavy, viscous substance.)

Horn-loaded enclosures and resonant types, such as the bass reflex, rely primarily on acoustical damping; direct-radiator systems on the electrical damping just described.

Multi-Speaker Systems

The construction requirements of loudspeakers are not the same for the different frequency ranges. Therefore the frequency spectrum is often divided up, by a *dividing network* or *cross-over network* between amplifier and speaker, into two, three, or even four parts, and each part is fed to a separate speaker system designed for that particular application. When the units are mounted together on the same physical axis the speaker is called *coaxial.*

A less expensive way of achieving a diversion of frequency and specialization of speakers is to create the division as a consequence of the mechanical characteristics of a particular speaker (such as allowing one section of the cone to vibrate at high frequencies), and to assign the different parts of the frequency spectrum to different parts of the same speaker rather than to different speakers.

Low-frequency speakers are referred to as *woofers,* high-frequency speakers as *tweeters;* these terms are by now generally accepted as part of audio technical language rather than audio slang.

Electrostatic Speakers

The electrostatic speaker uses the attraction and repulsion forces of electrostatic charges between plates, rather than electromagnetic forces. If two plates, closely spaced, are held parallel to each other as in *Fig.* 11–3(A), and one is allowed to move, they can be stimulated mechanically by varying the electrostatic charge between them. A fixed charge is placed on the stationary plate, and the signal is applied to the movable plate. This is called a single-ended system.

There is a difficulty, however. The force between the plates is a function of the charge, and of the square of the separating distance: thus as the plates move further apart the force is weakened, and as they move closer together

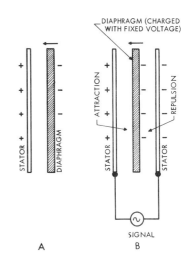

Fig. 11-3. (A) Basic elements of a "single-ended" electrostatic speaker. (B) Basic elements of a push-pull electrostatic speaker.

the force is increased, independently of the signal. The pattern of vibration will therefore not be an accurate replica of the pattern of the electrical input signal.

The solution to this distortion problem is to use a push-pull arrangement. In *Fig.* 11–3(B) we have two stationary plates instead of one, with the movable plate between: when the repelling force between the moving diaphragm and one "stator" is decreased by distance, a compensating increase in attracting force to the second stator is created by greater proximity.

The great advantage of the electrostatic speaker is that the diaphragm is driven uniformly over its surface, and tends to move without flexing or "breaking up," making possible uniformity of frequency response and low distortion.

Speaker Performance Characteristics

The most important performance

characteristics of loudspeakers relate to harmonic distortion, uniformity of frequency response (and the transient response associated therewith), frequency range, power handling capability, efficiency, and the directional pattern at the higher frequencies.

Distortion

High-quality loudspeakers are expected to keep harmonic distortion below one or two per cent, at an acoustic power output producing concert level in a relatively large room, over the frequency mid-range and upper bass. In the octave below 60 cps, however, distortion may be many times higher.

We have seen that intermodulation distortion can only be introduced when signals of different frequency are passed through the same distorting device. No matter what the harmonic distortion of a woofer, then, no intermodulation will be created with a treble signal which is reproduced by a separate tweeter. Furthermore, intermodulation test frequencies may be chosen so that the lower of the two frequencies is above the region where bass distortion becomes gross. In such a case the test results will not accurately reflect speaker distortion, even when both signals are reproduced by the same speaker. Until such matters have been standardized, then, a more reliable guide to speaker distortion is a graph which plots harmonic distortion percentage, at given acoustical output, over the frequency scale.

The subjective effects of speaker bass distortion can be detected readily with a little experience: the music takes on a muddy or wooden quality, especially when sustained, very low tones such as those from organ pedal pipes or bowed bass viols, appear. High-frequency distortion is associated with a strident, harsh effect.

Frequency Response and Dispersion

Loudspeakers show the same weaknesses in frequency-response characteristics as in distortion, if we compare their performance with amplifiers or pickups. Variation in power output is usually at least 5 db each side of reference level over the range reproduced, and sharp peaks and dips in the response curve are common.

Speaker frequency response information must be carefully qualified to have any meaning. The expression "frequency response from x to y cps" is especially meaningless for a loudspeaker.

Speaker bass response must be qualified by distortion data, or the "response" may refer almost entirely to the distortion products produced at given input frequencies. The writer was once present at an amateur demonstration of a loudspeaker whose bass response was supposed to extend to 20 cps. The demonstrator turned his audio signal generator on at 20 cps, and the loudspeaker "responded" vigorously, with a noise resembling machine-gun fire. Perhaps a tiny fraction of the sound was 20 cps energy: in any meaningful language this speaker could not have been described as having output at 20 cps. Its frequency range rating should have been restricted to that portion of the spectrum in which harmonic distortion was kept reasonably low.

While distortion output in the mid-range and treble does not normally rise to values high enough to affect the response curve, high-frequency speaker frequency response must be qualified in another way to have meaning. The on-axis response curve by itself ceases to have the significance that the bass on-axis curve did.

When we listen to a loudspeaker in a normally reverberant room we hear both direct sound, from the speaker to our ears, and reflected sound from the room surfaces. *The major part* of the sound that we hear is reflected. Thus, even if we are sitting on-axis to the speaker, we hear a total sound which is formed by the speaker's radiations in all directions.

Speaker off-axis response is often radically different from the on-axis response, mainly in that the treble falls off because of poor dispersion, and also in that smooth on-axis response may be accom-·panied by rough off-axis response. It is possible for two speakers to have very similar on-axis response curves and yet sound completely different in quality. A tweeter with smooth, on-axis response extending to 20,000 cps, for example, can have severely attenuated off-axis response except at the bottom of its range. This means that in the lower treble it radiates full energy, while in the higher treble the sound energy, restricted to a narrow beam, is greatly reduced. The sound can be nasal or "honky" because of concentration of energy in the mid-range, and lack any of the brilliance expected from extended response. It will be noted that a dispersing lens will spread out the deficient treble energy, but will not correct the basic deficiency of insufficient treble power response.

The smaller and stiffer the radiating diaphragm of a tweeter the better the dispersion and high-frequency power response to be expected.

Transient Response

There are two aspects of transient response: reproduction of the attack of a sound, and reproduction of the decay. A steady-state frequency response which is smooth and full-range predicts good performance on both counts: peaky response predicts "ringing" or hangover on decay, and attenuated mid- or high-frequency response detracts from the sharpness of the attack sound.

Consider the wave form of *Fig.* 11–4, for example. This is a simplification of the wave form of a sound that begins with a percussive attack and later ends abruptly; let us assume that this sound is to be reproduced through a woofer-tweeter system.

The attack is part of the cycle shown in dotted line, whose frequency is many times higher than the fundamental of the actual steady tone. This attack frequency may not even be reproduced by the woofer, but in any case has no relation to its low frequency performance.

On the other hand, when the tone stops the burden is being carried exclusively by the woofer. It, too, must stop abruptly, and not add any vibrations of its own for good measure.

Poor transient response in the decay of sound results in a "boomy" or "ringing" quality, making it difficult to distinguish the exact pitch of low-frequency tones. Poor transient response in attack, of either bass or treble sound, results in sound which is unnaturally dull.

Power Capability and Efficiency

Speakers are often rated according to the maximum number of electrical watts that are recommended for their use. This rating must be related to their electroacoustic efficiency, since the same electrical power into one speaker may produce as much as 30 times the

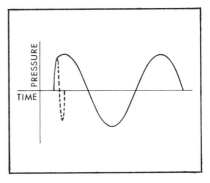

Fig. 11-4. Simplified wave form of a sound with percussive attack and abrupt decay. Transient response to the attack is a function of mid- or high-frequency speaker response: proper reproduction of the decay, without hangover, is associated with uniform low-frequency response.

actual sound power as into another. Speaker efficiencies range from one per cent or lower to perhaps 30 per cent (for horn-type systems), with five per cent a typical figure. Efficiency has no relationship to speaker quality, but inefficiency is a hidden cost, as it makes necessary an amplifier with higher power.

A more meaningful type of power "rating", from the point of view of reproduction in the home, is one which suggests the minimum amplifier power to be used with a particular speaker.

12.

SPEAKER ENCLOSURES

THE FUNCTION of the loudspeaker "motor" is to produce mechanical vibrations of the voice coil, corresponding to the acoustical vibrations of the original voice or music. When this has been done, however, the task of recreating the sound is far from completed. We must communicate the mechanical vibrations to the air, and the way in which we do this has a profound effect on the workings of the motor itself.

The voice coil, vibrating alone, can accomplish little in the way of radiating sound. It has no bite of the air, and even though it were to move back and forth vigorously it could do almost no useful acoustical work. It would be as ineffective as the shaft of an electric fan with the blades removed. And so we attach a diaphragm to the voice coil, to give it some air to work against.

But this does not wholly solve the problem, as anyone knows who has ever listened to an unmounted speaker sitting on a table. Even with its diaphragm, an unmounted loudspeaker reproduces very little bass. The cone becomes "decoupled" from the air of the room at lower frequencies, for reasons that we will examine in a moment. It is at these lower frequencies that the speaker mounting device or enclosure becomes indispensable; the primary function of the enclosure is to keep the diaphragm coupled to the air at the lower part of its frequency range.

There are three basic types of mounting device, each, of course, with variations on the basic theme. These three types may be categorized as the direct-radiator baffle, the resonant enclosure, and the horn.

The Direct-Radiator Baffle

When a speaker cone moves forward it simultaneously compresses the air in front of it and rarefies the air behind it. At high frequencies the wavelengths are short, and the cone itself acts to "baffle" or separate the front wave from the back wave. But at low frequencies the areas of compressed air in front of the cone are in direct contact with the areas of rarefied air at the back: the molecules of air hasten around the edges of the speaker to equalize things.

Thus the vibrating cone sets up a vibratory low-frequency wind around its edges, as illustrated in (A) of *Fig. 12–1*, but radiates little bass energy. The pressures and rarefactions in front of the cone are sapped by the opposite rarefactions and pressures behind it, and never get to work on the air of the room. This type of energy source is called a *doublet*—it has two parts, each radiating out of phase with the other, and cancelling the effects of its mate.

The solution to the doublet problem is quite simple—it is to insert an external baffle between the air in front of the speaker and the air behind it. In practical terms we saw a hole in a piece of rigid material, and mount the loudspeaker against the hole in such a way that it faces its audience through the opening. In this way the circulatory currents of air around the speaker edges are stopped, as illustrated in (B) of *Fig. 12–1*, and the pressures and rarefactions produced in front of the speaker can only move outward.

That is really all there is to it: the theoretical problem of preventing the speaker from losing its bite at lower frequencies is completely solved. The solution has its drawbacks from the practical point of view, but if the cone vibrates in an accurate replica of the input signal, simple baffling probably introduces the least amount of change in the conversion from mechanical to acoustical energy.

The practical problems involved relate to size, and to the fact that in a direct-radiator system the greatest burden is placed on the fidelity of the speaker mechanism: for a given sound output the cone has to move the farthest. There are three approaches to meeting these practical problems: wall mounting, use of a large, totally enclosed cabinet, and employment of the "acoustic suspension" system.

Wall Mounting

If we are to prevent interaction between the front and back of the cone successfully, the diameter of the baffle must be equal to at least half a wavelength at the lowest frequency that we are concerned with. This means that, for baffling a direct-radiator system down to 40 cps or so without losses, a baffle 14 feet across is required. The impracticality of such a piece of furniture is obvious.

However, such baffles are effectively

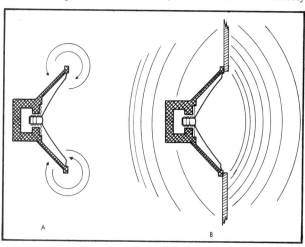

Fig. 12-1. (A) Interaction between front and back of an unmounted speaker. (B) Baffle prevents front and back waves from cancelling.

A

B

built into every house, in the walls between rooms, or those covering a stairwell or closet (provided the landlord is willing that they be considered as such). Wall mounting provides about as excellent and trouble-free a method of speaker "enclosure" as can be had. The rules that must be followed are relatively simple, compared to those for the more complicated enclosures. These rules are:

1. The speaker must not face into a tunnel-shaped opening, either forward or backward. Such an opening will tend to act like a resonant organ pipe, and will itself 'speak" its own tones in the upper bass.

2. The speaker must be securely anchored.

3. The rear of the speaker must not be enclosed by a volume of small dimensions (see the discussion following on totally enclosed cabinets).

One method of mounting a loudspeaker in a wall is illustrated in *Fig. 12–2.* When all of the conditions referred to are satisfied this type of mount is called an "infinite" baffle.

Totally Enclosed Cabinets

The characteristics of the infinite baffle may be closely imitated by the use of a totally enclosed cabinet. Here, as in the case of wall mounting, all interaction between the front and back of the speaker is prevented, but new problems are also introduced.

The most important of these new problems is the effect of the volume of air, enclosed by the cabinet, which the rear of the cone must compress and expand when it moves in and out. This volume of air constitutes a pneumatic spring, and it increases the spring tension of the speaker's mechanical system.

Now there is nothing wrong with spring tension in the mechanical system of the speaker. Such spring tension has, as a matter of fact, been built into the speaker, in the elastic suspensions used

to hold the cone and voice coil centered. These suspensions, as we have seen, partly determine the bass resonant frequency of the speaker's moving system.

But the proper amount of spring tension has been built into the speaker, and the resonant frequency is already as high as has been intended. (Although we would like the bass resonant frequency as low as possible there is a lower limit for a given speaker: too low an elastic restoring force in the suspensions permits the voice coil to travel beyond the range of uniform magnetic flux, and introduces distortion in the low bass.)

When the pneumatic spring of the cabinet's enclosed air is added to the mechanical springs of the speaker suspensions, the resonant frequency is raised. If the volume of air in the cab-

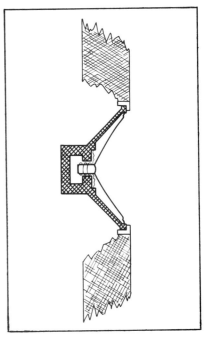

Fig. 12-2. Speaker mounted in a wall, avoiding pipe-shaped space formed by thickness of wall.

inet is very large[1] the pneumatic spring is weak and the effect is negligible; if the cabinet volume is too small the pneumatic spring is stiff, and the resonant frequency may be raised as much as an octave. We already know that we must expect bass attenuation, at 12 db/octave, below the resonant frequency. We thus stand to lose heavily in the bass unless our cabinet is of very large dimensions.

Other precautions that must be observed in using totally enclosed cabinets are:

1. The cabinet must be very rigid and vibration-proof. Three-quarter inch plywood, held together by screws and glue, and having ribs spaced about a foot apart, is one way of achieving this rigidity. Another method, that has been suggested by G. A. Briggs, is to use sand-filled panels.

2. The interior of the cabinet must be lined with sound absorbent material (such as Fiberglas in 4-inch thickness) to prevent standing waves and air-column resonances from forming within the cabinet. The enclosure must not act like a closed pipe.

It is interesting to note that the sound-absorbent material does not decrease the effective interior volume of the enclosure from the point of view of its pneumatic stiffness, but actually increases it. When the cabinet is *filled* with such material the effective elastic compliance or "give," and hence the effective cubic volume, may increase as much as 1.4 times. Filling the cabinet with Fiberglas also increases speaker damping at the bass resonance, and is usually a good idea. With some speakers, however, there is danger of overdamping and consequent bass attenuation.

[1]Conservative dimensions for totally enclosed cabinets are: 15-in. speaker, 15 cu. ft.; 12-in. speaker, 9 cu. ft.; 8-in. speaker, 4½ cu. ft. Reduction of these figures by 25 per cent or so does not usually involve much of a sacrifice.

The Acoustic Suspension System

The acoustic suspension system applies the infinite baffle principle to a special speaker-enclosure combination which is designed as a single unit. It is also called *air suspension,* since an air spring supplants the mechanical spring of the cone suspensions.

We have referred, in the chapter on loudspeakers, to the high values of bass harmonic distortion which are tolerated in speakers, compared to values considered as acceptable maxima in amplifiers and pickups. These high values of distortion are associated with two principal causes, both of which are related to the large excursions which the cone makes at low frequencies. (In the case of a direct-radiator the speaker cone must quadruple its distance of travel for each lower octave, if it is to keep up constant power output.) These are:

1. The voice coil tends to move out of the uniform magnetic field on large excursions, and the magnetic force is reduced at the peak of the cycle.

2. The mechanical speaker suspensions become non-linear on large excursions (they begin to "bind" in the axial direction, repressing cone movement on cycle peaks).

The first of these causes of distortion may be taken care of, in good bass speakers, by overhanging the voice coil past the magnetic gap. The voice coil may be made as much as ½ inch longer than the gap, so that even on large movements the same number of turns of copper wire is immersed in the magnetic field. Unfortunately a large sacrifice in electroacoustic efficiency follows.

The second factor—non-linear speaker suspensions—has been with us for years in spite of repeated redesign of these suspensions, and is thus the major single cause of bass distortion in speakers. The acoustic suspension speaker system cuts the Gordian knot rather than unravel-

[2]E. M. Villchur, U. S. Patent No. 2,775,309, Dec., 1956.

ling it—the suspensions are almost done away with.

The first design step is to eliminate most of the elastic tension of the mechanical suspensions, so that the speaker mechanical system is very loose. It can then be moved back and forth without having to overcome any appreciable mechanical spring tension. Only a small fraction of the normal elastic stiffness is built into the speaker (enough must be retained so that the voice coil can be centered in the gap without rubbing), and the resonant frequency of the unmounted speaker mechanism is usually subsonic.

This first step gives us a speaker which is, so to speak, a crippled unit. In a standard enclosure the voice coil would not be inhibited from travelling out of the bounds of its linear magnetic path, or even from "bottoming" against parts of the magnet structure, on high-power, low-frequency signals. It is an incomplete speaker.

The second step is to reintroduce the spring tension that has been removed. However, the spring that is introduced is pneumatic rather than mechanical; we use the enclosed air of a sealed, rigid, Fiberglas-filled enclosure. The same effect that was a problem previously—raising of the resonant frequency of the speaker due to the elastic stiffness of the enclosed air of the cabinet—is here used to give the system the characteristics that it needs. The pneumatic stiffness of the enclosure substitutes for the decimated mechanical stiffness of the speaker suspensions, and the resonant frequency of the total mechanical system is raised to the value that it would have had originally, if it had been designed in the conventional way.

The enclosed volume of air, compared to conventional speaker suspensions, is an almost ideal spring within the range of compression used, and does not create the non-linearity and distortion of the latter. Speaker bass harmonic dis-

tortion is thus radically reduced. In the octave below 60 cps particularly, this reduction may be expected to be of a large order.

Unlike the totally enclosed cabinet, in which there is no upper limit to the cubic volume of the enclosure for optimum performance, the acoustic suspension system requires a cabinet of just that volume which will raise the resonant frequency to its proper value. This means that for a given speaker mechanism there will be an *optimum* rather than *minimum* cabinet size. The optimum cabinet size is fortunately conveniently small—in the case of the existing commercial units built to this design it is about two cubic feet over-all. *Fig. 12–3* shows the difference between a

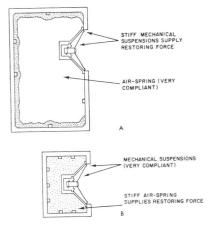

Fig. 12-3. (A) Totally enclosed speaker system. The major part of the speaker's restoring force is in the elastic stiffness of its mechanical suspensions. Cabinet volume is as large as possible, to prevent the stiffness of the air from having any effect. (B) Acoustic suspension system, showing substitution of air-spring to supply the bulk of restoring force. The speaker suspensions are much too compliant to perform this function. Other things being equal, the total elastic stiffness (and the final resonant frequency) is the same for each system, but the acoustic suspension system works on the more linear air-spring.

81

totally enclosed speaker system and an acoustic suspension speaker system.

It can be seen that the acoustic suspension system is not really a separate speaker and enclosure, and may be thought of as a loudspeaker whose outside material happens to be of wood.

It will be seen, in the section following, that there is an approach to reducing speaker distortion other than making the moving system linear for large excursions—that of reducing the excursion required for a given sound output.

We have seen that in direct-radiator speaker systems the function of the enclosure may be thought of as a negative one, separating front and back waves (except in the case of the acoustic suspension cabinet, which must also supply elastic restoring force to the speaker). In resonant and horn systems, however, the enclosure, in addition to serving as a baffle, plays a definite positive role in the radiation of bass frequencies.

Resonant Enclosures

It will be recalled that a Helmholtz resonator is that type of acoustical resonator in which an enclosed body of air, with an opening to the outside, vibrates as a mass-elasticity system—the cavity of air supplying the elasticity, and the air in the port providing the (acoustic) mass. The confined air is compressed and expanded uniformly, so that the device pulsates as a single unit rather than in sections, and it does not create overtones like those of an organ pipe. The sound produced by blowing across the mouth of an empty jug illustrates the pure fundamental output of the Helmholtz resonator, as compared to the rich harmonic spectrum of air column resonances.

Suppose we were to mount a speaker so that the cone faced into such a Helmholtz resonator, and the sound emerging into the listening room came from the resonator's port. The speaker would thus be radiating through the Helmholtz resonator rather than directly, and would of course be strongly influenced by the characteristics of the resonator.

This does not quite describe the design of the bass-reflex enclosure, but it is close. In the bass-reflex system only the rear of the speaker faces the room (acoustically speaking) through the Helmholtz resonator, and the front of the cone continues to act as a direct radiator. Furthermore the rear sound path, through the cabinet, becomes ineffective at the mid and high frequencies, where the front of the cone takes over and acts in the same way as in a purely direct-radiator system. The bass-reflex speaker system is illustrated in Fig. 12–4.

One might be led to believe that the cabinet resonator would "speak" almost continuously at its own natural frequency whenever it received energy from the speaker in this frequency region, adding an artificial, boomy quality to the music. This is, unfortunately, precisely what happens with improperly adjusted bass-reflex systems, and evidently the number of improperly adjusted systems has been great enough to create undeserved criticism of the

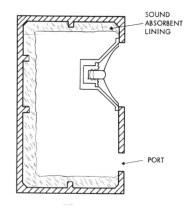

Fig. 12–4. Bass-reflex enclosure.

bass-reflex enclosure itself. A correctly designed bass-reflex enclosure, adjusted to the particular speaker used, is capable of producing clean, wide-range bass, and of extending the capabilities of the speaker used, particularly from the point of view of decreasing bass harmonic distortion.

The bass-reflex system is a combination, or *mesh*, of two resonant systems, the mechanical moving system of the speaker and the acoustical Helmholtz resonator. A detailed analysis of the behavior of resonant systems in mesh is not in order here, but the conclusion may be stated that the performance of the combination has qualities of its own. Specifically, when the resonant frequencies of the two systems are the same the single resonant peak is replaced by two smaller peaks, above and below the original resonant frequency, and when the proper amount of damping is applied, the smaller peaks may be "ironed out."

Thus when the Helmholtz resonator of the bass-reflex enclosure is tuned to the same resonant frequency as the speaker, and when the port is properly damped, instead of boomy, one-note low-frequency reproduction we may expect uniform, extended bass. Most important, the resonator increases the efficiency with which energy is coupled from the speaker to the air at low frequencies, and a given bass power can be radiated from the speaker (through the Helmholtz resonator) with smaller cone excursions. Since the non-linearity of speaker suspensions, as we have seen, is the major source of harmonic distortion, the decreased requirement for voice-coil excursion may radically reduce bass harmonic distortion.

Let us again resort to an analogy for the purpose of gaining an intuitive grasp of the physical working of the device we are investigating. Suspend a weight on a long rubber band. Holding on to the free end of the band, move

your hand up and down. It will be seen that at one frequency of vibration (the resonant frequency of the system) the weight will move the farthest. It can be made to travel over a much longer path than that over which your hand moves.

Two things may be noted; first, that at resonance the motion of the weight and of the hand applying the force are more or less in opposite directions —out of phase—and second, that at resonance the load imposed by the weight is greatest—one feels the greatest resistance. The hand doing the work represents the moving speaker cone; the weight represents the acoustical mass of the air in the enclosure's port, and the rubber band, communicating energy to the weight, represents the enclosed air of the cabinet. The "anti-resonance" of the acoustical system (which pulls or pushes *against* the force of the speaker) is thus illustrated. The speaker's coupling to the outside air (its "bite") in the resonance region is increased because small motions of the cone produce large motions of air in the port, just as small motions of the hand produced large motions of the suspended weight. *Fig.* 12–5 shows this mechanical analogy of weight and spring in place in the actual reflex cabinet.

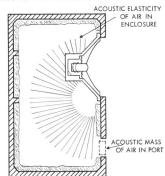

Fig. 12-5. Illustration of mass-elasticity system of bass-reflex Helmholtz resonator, and how it couples the rear of the speaker cone to the outside.

An improperly adjusted bass-reflex enclosure not only loses the advantages listed here, but introduces peaked characteristics of its own which create very unnatural, if loud, bass reproduction. Such a system is actually improved by stopping up the port opening. Methods of tuning and damping bass reflex enclosures to the particular speaker being housed involve changing the size of the port opening and stretching cloth across the opening for damping.

Other resonant enclosures are, for the most part, variations on the theme discussed above. The acoustical resonator may be an air column rather than of the Helmholtz type, as in the acoustical labyrinth and the "air coupler." Here there is an additional problem, of suppressing the harmonics of the column.

Horns

The basic purpose of a horn is to increase the coupling between a vibrating source of sound and the surrounding air. The horn is an ancient acoustical device, and loud blasts of sound, for military or other applications, could be produced thousands of years ago by persons who forced their lips to vibrate against the mouthpiece of a horn.

It is evident that, for a given vibratory excursion, the larger the radiating diaphragm the more air will be moved and the greater the sound energy that will be radiated. But large diaphragms are inconvenient and heavy. By using a flared transmission channel (a horn) the *effective* radiating area of a source of sound can be increased to that of the mouth, or large end.

Let us divide the air of a horn into imaginary successive layers, infinitesimally thin, each one a tiny bit greater in diameter than the last. (See *Fig. 12–6.*) When we stimulate the small diameter layer at the throat of the horn with sound we will progressively engage each of the succeeding layers of air. Because of the gradual change of diam-

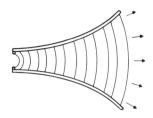

Fig. 12-6. Increase of effective radiating area of a small diaphragm at the throat of a horn to the area of the mouth.

eter (the "impedance discontinuity" between each successive layer is negligibly small) we will find that the source of sound at the throat engages all of the air in the horn. We can think of the horn as having an imaginary, massless diaphragm at the mouth, of much larger diameter than our real diaphragm, which is controlled by the latter. This "virtual" diaphragm is no less effective for being imaginary—the molecules of air are vibrating back and forth just as if a diaphragm the size of the horn's mouth were actually there.

There may appear to be an unreal quality about the action of a horn, in that it seems to get something for nothing, making a soft sound into a loud one. A horn is purely a passive device, and does not inject additional energy into the system. But the reason that a horn is able to increase so dramatically the radiation of sound from a given source (by factors of 10 or more) is that most sources of sound have only a very poor bite of the surrounding air, and do not succeed in changing much of their mechanical energy into acoustical energy. The horn allows the mechanical power capabilities of the source of sound to be tapped much more efficiently. In the case of a horn-loaded loudspeaker neither the electromechanical efficiency nor the power capability of the speaker itself is changed, but the transfer of mechanical to acoustical energy (the mechanico-acoustic efficiency of the system) is greatly increased. Capability for the extra power drawn from the system was there, unused, all the time.

The use of the horn in the development of sound reproducing equipment is illustrated in Fig. 12–7. The earlier horns were necessities, as the small diaphragms could not move far enough to produce anything like the required volume of sound. The modern bass horn illustrated in *D* is not a necessity, but is used to increase the efficiency of the speaker and to reduce the excursion re-

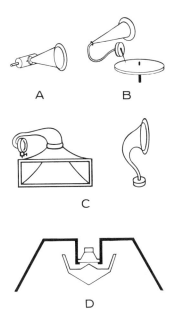

Fig. 12-7. Use of the horn as an acoustical coupler over the last seventy-five years (A) rigidly attached to phono pickup (Edison); (B) attached by flexible tubing (Berliner); (C) curved to conserve space; and (D) folded bass horn with dynamic speaker driver.

quirements of the speaker mechanism.

Horns have their special problems, too. There are two characteristics of horns as transmitters of sound energy that are especially significant: the cutoff frequency, and the formation of standing wave resonances due to reflections from the mouth, as in an openended organ pipe.

Below a certain frequency, determined by the rate of flare, the horn ceases to act as an efficient sound coupler. To keep the cut-off frequency low, the rate of flare of the horn must be very gradual. This characteristic is independent of the actual length of the horn, but if we want a large mouth the slow flare must be continued over a long distance. And it is important that the mouth be large, for reasons other than those relating to efficiency. Unless the mouth is large enough (the absolute size required is related to how low the frequencies to be reproduced are) the mouth reflections and standing wave resonances become great.

A slow flare and a large mouth add up to a very large structure. If we put numbers into these general relationships we will find that, for a horn conveying fairly uniform bass down to low frequencies, we will have a piece of furniture that we cannot use in a living room, let alone get through the door. This problem was met by the Klipschorn, which folded the horn path back onto itself and then, being placed in a corner, used the walls of the room as an extension of the flared paths.

Both horns and resonant type enclosures decrease the burden placed on the speaker compared to direct-radiator baffle systems, particularly from the point of view of the voice-coil excursion required at low frequencies. They also bring with them their own resonances, which must be strictly tamed for high-quality reproduction.

13.

ROOM ENVIRONMENT

LIKE THE WEATHER, room acoustics is a subject which is talked about but seldom acted upon. There are, of course, many situations in which the builder of a sound reproducing system lacks either the power or the authority to take measures relative to the acoustical environment of the room (hi-fi wives being as they are—justifiably). But there are also principles than can be followed which, without turning things upside down, are able to improve significantly the performance of an installation in a given room.

Position of the Speaker System

If a speaker were mounted in an infinite, non-absorbent wall it would look out on half the universe. If it were placed at the junction of two such walls it would "see" only a quarter of the universe, and at the junction of three walls it would be restricted to servicing one-eighth of the universe. We may refer to these conditions as the speaker seeing, or radiating into, a solid angle of 180 deg., 90 deg., and 45 deg., respectively.

The dimensions of a living room are

not infinite, but the analogy to mounting a speaker system mid-wall, at the junction of floor and wall, and in a corner on the floor (or at the ceiling), should be evident. These three positions, in the order mentioned, progressively restrict the speaker's solid angle of radiation.

In the case of the infinite restricting surfaces it is obvious that when the solid angle is decreased the sound radiated by the speaker is concentrated, and a given amount of power will create higher sound pressures at a given distance from the source. In our room, however, the same cubic volume has to be filled with sound no matter where we place the speaker. We can properly ask, therefore, whether the solid angle of radiation makes a difference in room performance.

The answer is that it makes a profound difference. If the solid angle of radiation is restricted by mounting position, air cannot fall away from the cone in all directions. Cone-to-air coupling is increased greatly at bass frequencies, but higher frequency sound has already been restricted in its dispersion by the nature of radiating diaphragms. Mid-range and treble "bite" is thus unaffected.

The differences in bass response which result from varying the mounting position of the speaker system may be greater than those which exist between different brands of speakers. The change from mid-wall to three-sided corner mounting will increase the relative bass power four times (6 db). *Fig.* 13–1 illustrates the difference in frequency response, for a particular speaker, associated with four types of mounting position. The dotted line is for the speaker in the actual center of the room, on a pedestal or dangling by a rope. Here the loss of bass power, compared to that from a three-sided corner, is by a factor of 8, or 9 db.

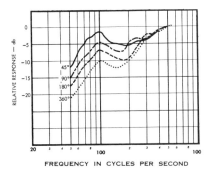

FREQUENCY IN CYCLES PER SECOND

Fig. 13-1. Frequency response of the same speaker system at four different solid angles of radiation. (A) Corner of room, on floor (45 deg); (B) junction of floor and mid-wall (90 deg); (C) mid-wall (180 deg); (D) suspended at center of room (360 deg). (After Beranek)

What we have shown is that a corner mounting position, on the floor or at the ceiling, provides the fullest bass. This does not imply that such a mounting position is optimum for all rooms or for all speaker systems. A system (or room) that tends to be bass-heavy, for example, will be improved if the speaker is taken out of the corner, or raised off the floor. A floor position may also be less than

optimum from the point of view of the treble; it is not normally desirable for the treble speaker to be low. Keeping the speaker enclosure cater-cornered, but several feet off the floor, is often an excellent compromise in monaural systems.

Placement of Stereo Speakers

Stereo speakers are generally placed six to ten feet apart, larger rooms calling for the greater spacing. They can be placed symmetrically (woofers on the inside, tweeters on the outside, or vice versa) or asymmetrically; one setup is as good as the other. The speakers are usually mounted facing the same way, but in some rooms they work well if they are turned outward, at right angles to each other.

A corner mounting is usually (not always) less desirable in stereo. The two speakers tend to give each other bass reinforcement, and since the position of the second speaker is tied to that of the first, corner mounting is liable to pull the area commanded by the speakers to one side.

Room Liveness

A room is "live" when it is very reverberant; it is called dead when the reverberation is very much subdued. When one enters a room the sound of footsteps, conversation, etc., take on a characteristic quality,—a ring or a dullness associated with the acoustical environment of that room. The relative liveness of the room can also be tested roughly by listening to the sound of a sharp hand-clap, and noting the length of time required for the sound to die away. The longer the time the more reverberant the room.

The tonal balance of the output of an ideal reproducing system may be destroyed by a room which is too live or too dead acoustically. Dead rooms tend to over-absorb the higher frequencies (especially the mid-highs) relative to the bass, giving the sound a dull, muffled character. A room that is too live has the opposite effect, and may be conducive to over-bright sound with an accentuated treble—the sound may even appear strident.

Smooth wood or plaster surfaces, bare walls and floors, etc., tend to create a live room, while drapes, rugs, upholstered furniture and the like work to decrease liveness. The absorptive qualities of different materials commonly found in the home is listed in Table 13–2. There are special "acoustical" materials which are very effective in noise control work, but which are generally totally unsuitable for musical listening rooms. Their absorption vs. frequency characteristics tend to impart a very unnatural quality to reproduced music—unnatural in the sense that they introduce a coloration radically different from that imposed on the instruments by a more natural environment.

Once the room liveness has been established, and corrective measures applied as best they can be, the operator of a high-fidelity system has recourse to his tone controls and tweeter level controls. The neutral position for bass and treble tone controls may very well represent acoustical *imbalance* in particular circumstances. Occasionally high fidelity enthusiasts have been misled to believe that, for the purist, the function of tone controls is public display in their neutral position. Actually, tone controls are a powerful means of getting the characteristics of the reproducing system and of the room to complement each other.

Treble Dispersion

It was pointed out in the beginning of the chapter that the nature of radiating surfaces is to restrict the dispersion of sound as the frequency increases. Since the higher the frequency the less diffuse the pattern, there is a tendency for speaker sound to confine itself to an increasingly narrow beam as the frequency goes up (see *Fig.* 13–3). Listeners sitting on axis receive the full blast of the concentrated treble, while listeners seated off-axis tend to lose the treble portion of the spectrum.

This characteristic may be relieved in many ways, and high-fidelity speakers should have good dispersion patterns. Nevertheless it is difficult to avoid some narrowing in the treble, especially the upper portion, and the speaker should be placed so that it commands the room well. The corner placement discussed previously with regard to bass also serves in this connection.

It would obviously be wrong, for example, to face a speaker away from the major listening area and directly into a very absorptive surface, unless one

Fig. 13-2. Absorption coefficients of various materials commonly found in the home.

Material	Frequency, cps					
	128	256	512	1024	2048	4096
	Coefficient of Absorption					
Draperies hung straight, cotton fabric, 10 ounces/square yard, in contact with wall:	.04	.05	.11	.18	.30	.44
Draperies, velour, 18 ounces/square yard:	.05	.12	.35	.45	.40	.44
Velour draperies as above, 4" from wall:	.09	.33	.45	.52	.50	.44
.4" carpet on 1/8" felt on concrete:	.11	.14	.37	.43	.27	.27
.4" carpet on concrete:	.09	.08	.21	.26	.27	.37
Concrete, unpainted:	.01	.012	.016	.019	.023	.035
.5" plaster, lime on wood lath on wood studs, rough finish:	.039	.056	.061	.089	.054	.070
.5" plaster, gypsum:	.023	.039	.039	.052	.037	.035
Wood sheeting, pine, .8":	.10	.11	.10	.08	.08	.11

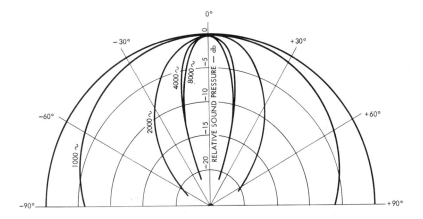

Fig. 13-3. Theoretical radiation pattern of 12-in. speaker (ignoring cone break-up) at different frequencies. A smaller speaker would have much better treble dispersion characteristics. (Courtesy Jensen Mfg. Co. — from Jensen Technical Monograph No. 1)

meant purposely to tone down the treble. Treble dispersion may be improved, however, by placing the speaker so that the sound impinges upon reflecting surfaces, and is reflected back to the listening area in the desired diffuse condition. This placement is particularly applicable when the speaker tends to be over-bright.

Acoustical Resonances of Listening Room

The most annoying and difficult-to-deal-with characteristics of listening rooms are their resonances. The hand-clap test referred to can also be used to help detect room resonance—an echo which has a fairly distinct musical pitch indicates a sharp resonance, and probably an unpleasant effect on reproduced music.

Not only is the reproduced sound accentuated at the frequencies of sharp room resonances, but the same "ringing" effect that followed the hand-clap influences the musical sound. The distinctness of orchestral or choral voices and the purity and accuracy of their tone colors is impaired or even ruined. The

quality of such reproduction was well described by Shakespeare's monster Caliban, who complained:

"Sometimes a thousand twangling instruments will hum about mine ears. . . ." thus prophecying the era of high fidelity shows.

A room with sharp resonances may be expected to yield a boomy bass and an unclear treble. A reproducing system with smooth frequency response may sound as though it has a peaky and ragged curve. Furthermore this is the acoustical condition for which it is hardest to correct.

Mounting the speakers at the end of a long, narrow room tends to strengthen room resonance more than if the speakers are mounted against the long wall. On the other hand mounting them against the long wall tends to lessen the bass, and the listener must decide which position gives the most natural effect. The best evaluative tool available to the high fidelity listener is a fresh memory of the sound of live music in the concert hall.

It is possible to experiment with placing absorptive surfaces in the room, particularly in such a way as to break up room patterns of regular geometry, as a method of counteracting acoustical resonance. Where there is a sharp resonance formed between two parallel walls, for example (as revealed by the hand-clap test) a drape hung on one of the walls may clear up the difficulty. The most practical way to deal with the problem, however, is to try different mounting positions for the speaker, a procedure which may force us to ignore conclusions arrived at by consideration of the other factors referred to earlier. The guidance principle is simple: if the sound has greater clarity and less unnatural reverberation in a particular position, that position is superior.

The best mounting position is the one that frees us to the greatest extent from the acoustical environment of the listening room. The goal is not to bring the musical instruments into the room, but to transport the listener to the concert hall.

There is normally nothing that can be done about relative room dimensions, but it is useful to know what to expect from different room shapes. The most annoying resonances are formed in rooms whose length, width, and height are the same or a simple multiple of each other.

Ideal room dimension ratios of height, length, and width are approximately 1:1.25:1.6 (the exact multiple is the cube root of 2). When room dimensions are so ordered the resonances are most evenly distributed over the frequency spectrum. Most rooms will have something in between the ideal ratios and the cubical form. The closer the ratios to the ideal, the more suitable the room can be expected to be for musical listening.

The room is the final transmission channel in the sound reproducing system, and one of the most aberrant. Intelligent tailoring of the system to the room should thus play an important part in the successful installation of reproducing equipment.

INDEX